THE WORKS OF TED HUGHES

LETTERS

LETTERS OF TED HUGHES
(selected and edited by Christopher Reid)

POETRY

THE HAWK IN THE RAIN

LUPERCAL

WODWO

CROW

GAUDETE

MOORTOWN

MOORTOWN DIARY

FLOWERS AND INSECTS

WOLFWATCHING

RAIN-CHARM FOR THE DUCHY

THREE BOOKS: Remains of Elmet,
Cave Birds, River

ELMET (with photographs by Fay Godwin)

NEW SELECTED POEMS 1957–1994

TALES FROM OVID

BIRTHDAY LETTERS

COLLECTED POEMS

SENECA'S OEDIPUS

WEDEKIND'S SPRING AWAKENING

LORCA'S BLOOD WEDDING

RACINE'S PHÉDRE

THE ORESTEIA OF AESCHYLUS

ALCESTIS

SELECTED POEMS OF EMILY DICKINSON

SELECTED VERSE OF SHAKESPEARE

THE RATTLE BAG
(edited with Seamus Heaney)

THE SCHOOL BAG
(edited with Seamus Heaney)

PROSE

POETRY IN THE MAKING

A DANCER TO GOD

SHAKESPEARE AND THE GODDESS OF
COMPLETE BEING

WINTER POLLEN: OCCASIONAL PROSE

DIFFICULTIES OF A BRIDEGROOM

FOR CHILDREN

HOW THE WHALE BECAME

MEET MY FOLKS!

THE EARTH-OWL AND OTHER MOON
PEOPLE

NESSIE, THE MANNERLESS MONSTER

THE COMING OF THE KINGS

THE IRON MAN

MOON-WHALES

SEASON SONGS

UNDER THE NORTH STAR

FFANGS THE VAMPIRE

BAT AND THE KISS OF TRUTH

TALES OF THE EARLY WORLD

THE IRON WOMAN

THE DREAMFIGHTER AND OTHER
CREATION TALES

COLLECTED ANIMAL POEMS, Vols. 1–4

THE MERMAID'S PURSE

THE CAT AND THE CUCKOO

COLLECTED POEMS FOR CHILDREN
(illustrated by Raymond Briggs)

TED HUGHES
Selected Translations

TED HUGHES (1930–98) produced more than forty books of poetry, prose, drama, translation and children's literature, including, in his last decade, *Shakespeare and the Goddess of Complete Being*, *Tales from Ovid* and *Birthday Letters*.

DANIEL WEISSBORT founded *Modern Poetry in Translation* with Ted Hughes. Until 1999, he directed the Translation Program at the University of Iowa. He is now an honorary professor at the Centre for Translation at the University of Warwick.

SELECTED
TRANSLATIONS

TED HUGHES

SELECTED TRANSLATIONS

Edited by Daniel Weissbort

FARRAR, STRAUS AND GIROUX

NEW YORK

FARRAR, STRAUS AND GIROUX
18 West 18th Street, New York 10011

Printed in the United States of America
Originally published in 2006 by Faber and Faber Limited, Great Britain
Published in 2007 in the United States by Farrar, Straus and Giroux
First American paperback edition, 2008

Owing to limitations of space, all acknowledgements for permission to reprint
previously published and unpublished material can be found on pages 235–37.

The Library of Congress has cataloged the hardcover edition as follows:
Selected translations / Ted Hughes ; edited by Daniel Weissbort.
    p. cm.
    Includes bibliographical references and index.
    ISBN-13: 978-0-374-26068-2 (hardcover : alk. paper)
    ISBN-10: 0-374-26068-0 (hardcover : alk. paper)
    1. Poetry—Translations into English.   I. Hughes, Ted, 1930–1998.
II. Weissbort, Daniel.

PN6101. S447 2006
808.81—dc22

               2007021367

Paperback ISBN-13: 978-0-374-53145-4
Paperback ISBN-10: 0-374-53145-5

www.fsgbooks.com

1   3   5   7   9   10   8   6   4   2

Contents

Introduction

Ted Hughes (1930–98), British Poet Laureate from 1984, was among the most important poetry translators in the English tradition. His interest in translation predates his 1965 co-founding of *Modern Poetry in Translation* (*MPT*), but the journal fed that interest, helping to bring a number of poets to his attention: notably the Israeli Yehuda Amichai, the Hungarian János Pilinszky and the Serbian Vasko Popa. Poems by the first two of these he translated and the last he did much to promote. In his early projects, involving collaboration with Peter Brook (Seneca's *Oedipus*, and *Orghast*), he gave evidence, however, of a deeper, philosophical commitment to translation.

One impulse for *Modern Poetry in Translation*, a project Hughes had already envisaged when he was in America in the late 1950s, had been his encounter with poets from Eastern Europe at various international festivals, and he remained interested in post-war East European poetry, particularly that of the generation immediately preceding his own, the circumstances of whose lives 'had brought their poetry down to such precisions, discriminations and humilities that it is a new thing'.[1] Hence also the allure of the English versions produced by the Israeli poet Yehuda Amichai of his own Hebrew poems, or of the scrupulously literal renderings and minutely annotated versions from the Hungarian of János Pilinszky by another Hungarian poet, János Csokits. Hughes was impressed by the way these auto-translations, as it were, conveyed the urgency of the original vision, which for him seemed often to be dissipated in more polished or, as we might now say, 'domesticated' versions.

Hughes's approach to the translation of poetry suggests a belief in the intrinsic ability of poetry to cross language frontiers, provided the translator does not interpose himself overmuch. The act of translation required not only intense listening but also a high degree of self-discipline. Nor, it should be added, did Hughes much trust critical commentary, unless, perhaps, as a supplement to a 'literal' version, as in the case of Vladimir Nabokov's polemical translation-plus-commentary of Pushkin's *Eugene Onegin*. That Hughes's interest in translation was no passing phase is evidenced by his continuing involvement in translation projects throughout his writing life. Although he took no part in the discussions, he may fairly be said to have subscribed to a foreignising tendency, a renewed readiness to allow translation of foreign texts to alter English itself, increasingly the world lingua franca. But more immediately, Hughes's involvement is surely related to his own needs as a writer and, as such, it provides additional clues to his development which have not yet received sufficient attention. It *has* been observed about his translations that, paradoxically, while intentionally remaining close to the ad verbum text, he nevertheless created works, maybe secondary, but unmistakably 'Hughesian'. However, that his translations *were* an integral part of his own oeuvre, just as the promotion of translation was perceived by him as part of his professional duty as a writer, seems largely to have been ignored.

One is reminded by, for example, his letter to Gaia Servadio (see page 99) of the extent to which Hughes hoped for and needed literal versions to activate his own poetic imagination. He was also aware of how difficult it was to obtain these, one reason for his so valuing the partnership with Csokits, who understood this need and provided Hughes with what he wanted: word-for-word or interlinear cribs plus linguistic and contextual information. It was, however, sometimes awkward asking for this kind of primary text, since interpreters tend to see such work as demeaning. Hughes came to appreciate this and exercised a good deal of tact when requesting such texts, making it clear how much he valued this material and how indebted he was to those who provided it, to the extent even of regarding his own contributions as secondary (see, for instance, his remarks about his role in the translation of Pilinszky's poetry: 'the troubled mechanic, rather than the co-pilot'). In addition, of course, there was the living connection with the poet himself/herself or with an appropriate source-language representative of the poet (Csokits, Servadio), supplying the indispensable immediate contact with the material and its actual sound.

Though comments and remarks on translation are to be found here and there in his writings, Hughes wrote only one short (uncollected) essay on the subject (see Appendix 1), describing the translation boom of the previous decade, while at the same time tentatively reformulating his bias towards literal translation. He refers in it to a work that for him represented a kind of model, *Specimens of Bushmen Folklore*, a collection made in the 1870s by the German-trained ethnographer and philologist William Bleek: 'Ideally we [the editors of *Modern Poetry in Translation*] would have liked to see at least some poems translated [. . .] as meticulously as Bleek's translation of Bushmen lore – though we understood the limited appeal of anything so raw and strange.' As in the early *Modern Poetry in Translation* editorials (see Appendix 1), Hughes inveighs against translations that aimed to produce a 'parallel equivalent of some original's unique verbal texture'. He comments that 'we found the closest thing to it [to what was wanted] in translations made by poets whose first language was not English [e.g., Czesław Miłosz's versions of poems by fellow Pole Zbigniew Herbert], or by scholars who did not regard themselves as poets'.

Hughes had to contend, in a sense, with his own talent. It would have been easier no doubt for him to imitate himself, his first outstandingly successful productions. Instead, he constantly attempted to transcend this verbal brilliance and dexterity, in his quest for something more basic, a regenerative form of words. About *Gaudete* (1977), for instance, he wrote to me: 'I once wrote a film scenario about a priest who turns all the women of his parish into his coven [. . .] I just re-wrote it, much altered, in a sort of verse, very crude lead-pipe verse [. . .] He gets killed at the end but then resurrects and writes a lot of poems which I quite like. They started being vacanas – as in that *Speaking of Shiva* book[2] – but then took off on their own.' Hughes seemed to be moving towards an elemental language, in a way replicating the development of certain European poets of the first post-war generation. Of these, János Pilinszky seemed closest to him. Pilinszky had experienced the war, but also made it his own, as distinct, for instance, from Różewicz, Holub or Herbert. What Pilinszky called his 'lack of language' was attributed by him to his learning it from a brain-damaged aunt. In other words, he attributed the sparseness of his diction, in the first place, to something in his personal biography rather than to the extreme conditions that he had witnessed and that cast doubts on language as such. Hughes, who was a little younger and who lived out the war in the relative security of England, could nevertheless identify with these concerns. It was also his good fortune, of course, to have on hand a Hungarian friend, fellow-poet, contemporary and admirer of Pilinszky, János Csokits.

Interestingly, Hughes's Pilinszky translations[3] did not meet with a positive response in the States. His American editor turned the collection down, the reasons relating precisely to Hughes's translation method, which was felt to have straitjacketed him. Hughes was bemused by this, but not deterred. His Introduction to the Pilinszky volume is a remarkable statement, as challenging today as it was when he wrote it, and could stand as a credo for 'foreignisation' as against 'domestication' or naturalising translation. I believe that Hughes's later translation of Classical and neo-Classical work (Ovid's *Metamorphoses*, Seneca's *Oedipus* and Racine's *Phèdre*, as well as plays by Aeschylus and Euripides) represents a development of this 'literalistic' approach. To return to Pilinszky, here is Hughes himself on the subject:

Very many lines of his [Csokits's] rough draft have been impossible to improve, as far as I could judge [. . .]. As it happens, the very thing that attracted me to Pilinszky's poems in the first place was their air of simple helpless accuracy. Nothing conveys that so well as the most literal crib, and I suppose if we had the audacity that is what we should be printing here. As it is, we settled for literalness as a first principle.

It is surely interesting, too, that Hughes evidently regarded his translations of Pilinszky's poetry as being at least as effective as his own work, which indicates a good deal of optimism regarding the ability of translation, at least in certain instances, to convey the essence of the original.

Hughes's notion of the literal did not engage with contemporary debates about 'domestication' (seen as a 'colonialistic' enterprise, seeking to make familiar and palatable what is *other*), nor with notions of 'foreignisation' (which emphasise the shock of the unfamiliar). Rather, it seems to have had to do with his belief that the irreducible minimum, the essential content or wisdom of foreign or remote texts, might be conveyed through scrupulous attention to the means of expression, sometimes even through painstakingly literal translations. In this connection, though he did not put it so polemically, he found Nabokov's views very much to his taste; Nabokov went so far as to assert that the only real translation was a literal crib.

So, what, finally, did draw Hughes to translation? As this collection suggests, his work as a translator parallels his other work and can even be seen as signalling various turns in its development. His encounter, for instance, with the poets of post-war Europe, especially of Eastern Europe, helped him to enlarge an existing preoccupation with the historical dilemma of the West, deepening his identification with World War I and with the poets of both world wars. Later, his immersion in

Classical drama, and the translation or reworking of some of its most important themes, extended his awareness of the possibilities of the theatre, particularly of its mythic dimension. His collaboration with Peter Brook is notable in this respect, culminating in an attempt, one might say, to bypass existing language altogether and to create, with *Orghast*, a language of direct communication.

It should also be pointed out that Hughes took his responsibilities, as he saw them, very seriously. It was this that led him, in the first place, to found the magazine *Modern Poetry in Translation* and to promote and direct the first Poetry International readings in London. But he was willing also to put himself and his poetic reputation on the line, translating two of the major poets of the generation preceding his own, János Pilinszky and Yehuda Amichai. In short, then, translation should be seen as an integral part of Hughes's creative and professional life. There are numerous links – I have suggested some above – between his work as a translator and what may be regarded as his own work. It is surely not paradoxical that both were his *own* work.

A word about the organisation of this volume. I have made selections from all of Hughes's major projects, both published and unpublished, and have placed these in chronological order, since I believe they should be considered in the context of his work as a whole. I hesitated over *Orghast*, Hughes's retelling of the Prometheus myth in a language invented by himself, since clearly this remarkable work in printed form requires a considerable apparatus. However, in view of its importance in Hughes's development as a writer and its relevance to his approach to translation and to language in general, I have attempted to represent it in the form of an essay for the most part, embodying comments by others, including Hughes himself.

Hughes's consistency is such that the selection presented here may also, I hope, be enjoyed in a similar way to a selection of his own verse. I have included in the Appendices additional material that the reader may find of interest or use, such as excerpts from correspondence, from other writings by Hughes, and excerpts from some of the texts which he made use of in producing his own versions. In the meantime, at the very least, the commitment of so major a poet to translation should not pass unnoticed.

Daniel Weissbort

NOTES

1. Introduction to *Vasko Popa: Collected Poems* (1978).
2. *Speaking of Shiva* (Penguin Classics, 1973), a collection of *vacanas* by some major tenth-century saint poets, translated by the poet/scholar, the late A. K. Ramanujan.
3. *János Pilinszky: Selected Poems*, translated by Ted Hughes and János Csokits, first published by Carcanet (1976) and re-published by Anvil Press as *The Desert of Love* (1989) in a revised and enlarged edition.

SELECTED
TRANSLATIONS

Bardo Thödol

The circumstances, as far as can be ascertained, are as follows. Ted Hughes and Sylvia Plath had gone to America in 1957 and the couple spent autumn 1959 in the artists' colony at Yaddo, Saratoga Springs, where Hughes worked on *Lupercal*. It was here that he met the Chinese-American composer Chou Wen-chung, who invited him to write the text for an opera he was planning, based on the *Bardo Thödol*, known as *The Tibetan Book of the Dead*. This ancient Tibetan manual had been translated by W. Y. Evans-Wentz, a version according to Lama Kazi Dawa-Samdup's English rendering. The Evans-Wentz translation was first published by Oxford University Press in 1927, the second edition appearing in 1949 and the third in 1957, one of these being in Hughes's possession.

The text was first put into written form by the legendary Padma Sambhava in the eighth century A D. 'Bardo Thödol' means 'liberation by hearing on the after-death plane'. The book is a guide for the dead during the state that is held to intervene between death and the next rebirth. It was traditionally read aloud to the dying to help them attain liberation, guiding the deceased and encouraging them to use the moment of death to recognise the nature of mind and attain liberation. It seeks to persuade its readers that both the peaceful and the terrifying, wrathful visions appearing at this time are their own creation, the result of gathered karma, or of actions followed by inevitable results. *The Tibetan Book of the Dead* teaches how one may attain liberation from the endless cycle of birth and rebirth, i.e., of cyclic suffering. The 'Light of Pure Reality', which it is hoped will be attained, is the 'true Intellect', inseparable from the 'Great Body of Radiance' or the 'mind of the Buddha'.

Professor Chou Wen-chung writes that there was considerable interaction between himself and Hughes over a period of time. The work, 'for musical and staging reasons', is not, in the composer's view, a translation as such, since the complexity of the source text necessitated a degree of condensation. The composer confirms that the text used was the Evans-Wentz translation, which may have been introduced to Hughes by himself, although it is also possible that Hughes first encountered it before, perhaps even when he was a student at Cambridge in the early 1950s, since 'he had already done some work on the *Bardo*'. Not surprisingly for such a large-scale project, and considering the status of the source, the text remained active for Hughes throughout his life, so that he was, in fact, contemplating a return to it shortly before his death, writing to the composer to that effect. That this did not happen means that the text has remained as it was initially conceived in 1959. It has yet to be published in its entirety.

Hughes worked for some six months on his *Bardo* text and it relates discernibly to a number of other writings (see in particular *Wodwo*, 1967). In connection with his radio-play 'The Wound' (included in *Wodwo*), Hughes, in a radio interview at the Adelaide Festival in March 1976 (transcribed by Ann Skea), conversationally commented: 'Well, it was a freak production really. At the time I was writing a scenario of the *Bardo Thödol – Tibetan Book of the Dead* [. . .] and at the end of it I had a dream, which was the dream of "The Wound" . . . much, much more complicated than the play as it is now . . . Well it was just like a full-length play, with many scenes, many things going on, but along with it was a full text. So I dreamed the action of the play, and was in the play, but simultaneously dreamed a very full text. And came out of the dream and woke up – and in the dream, this play had been written by John Arden – do you know *Sergeant Musgrave's Dance*? It must have been some memory of that.' Later in the same interview, he remarked of the play and his dream: 'I interpreted it first of all as a sort of Celtic *Bardo Thödol* – a Gothic *Bardo Thödol* – because, in fact, it's full of all the stock imagery of a journey to the Celtic underworld . . .' In spite of his casual, even somewhat self-deprecatory style, Hughes also offers some insight into the origins of his *Bardo* text and its connection with his work in general, special attention being paid to his fascination with the arduous and terrifying shamanistic journey.

Broadly speaking, translation for Hughes could either be what might be described as adaptation, based on a prolonged engagement with a major text, or a kind of literalism, as aimed at, for instance, in his translations of János Pilinszky and Yehuda Amichai, where his model, if he can be said to have had one, is Bleek's transcriptions and English versions of Bushmen folklore (see Introduction to the present volume). These apparently divergent aims, on the one hand free adaptation and on the other literal transcription, converge or are combined in his later adaptations of Classical Greek drama (the *Oresteia* and *Alcestis*). With the *Bardo* text, possibly because this was part of a joint project for an opera, or because the material was so culturally remote, Hughes's work can be described as relating to and involving translation, rather than as translation as such. It is included here because of its intrinsic merit and also because of its evident significance for Hughes himself.

The following excerpts are from Part One of the Hughes text. See Appendix 2 for some examples of the Evans-Wentz translation, which Hughes consulted.

CAST
Chorus A & B: Readers of the Thödol, Guide and Instructor
Chorus C: Relatives, Karmic Voices, etc.
Solo: Dead Soul

Excerpt 1

A: To the Divine Body of the Truth obeisance
A & B: The boundless incomprehensible light.
A: To the Divine Body of Perfect Endowment, obeisance. To the
   lotus-born Incarnation, Padma Sambhava, obeisance.
A & B: Protector of all things living
A: To the Gurus, the Three Bodies, obeisance.
C: (*Wail, as mourners. Then, as they fade:*)
A: Death comes over him slowly.
   Now earth drinks up the throb of his arteries,
   Earth drinks up the light of the world
   And his eyes darken, his mind darkens.
   This is: the moment for which his life has waited.
C: (*Wail, as mourners.*)
A: O Buddhas and Bodhisattvas, O you Compassionate
      Ones
   Endowed with knowledge, with the Divine Eye and with
      Perfect Love,
   Endowed with infinite powers of protection,
   Receive these offerings mentally created;
   Regard this man who is passing alone from the world.
B: Be with him in the long tormenting corridor of the Bardo.
C: (*Wail, as mourners.*)
A: The world ceases for him and he must go elsewhere.
   Alone, with naked foot, he enters a darkness
   Where all limits are in Dissolution.
   He leaps without friends,
   In misery without light,
   Without defenders, without protectors,
   Without weapons, without kinsmen,
   Into the circles of confusion
   Where the winds of Karma rustle and await him.

[3]

B: Protect him in the gloom and anguish of the Bardo.

C: (*Wail, as mourners.*)

A: The spirit of affliction has fastened upon him,
The messengers of death have fastened upon him.
His gathering of Karma, past pride and past
brutishness,
Past passionate attachments, to person, to self, to
possessions,
Like a starved beast runs again and again to birth with
him,
And again and again hurries him to death.
His misery is without light.
The time has come when he must go on alone.

C: (*Wail, as mourners.*)

A & B: O Dharma Kaya, Divine Body
Of Perfect Enlightenment
O Sambhoga Kaya, Divine Body
Of Perfect Endowment
O Nirmana Kaya, Divine
Body of Incarnation
Gather him into your Trinity in the Bardo.

A: Save him in the Bardo.

B: Raise him from the Bardo.

A & B: Let him escape forever the Wheel of Blood.

A: Now comes the sinking of earth into water.
Now the Bardo of his death's moment
Dawns as the world darkens.

B: Let him be placed in Perfect Buddhahood.

A: Abandoning desire, now let him enter the shining
Space of the Bright Teachings undistracted.

B: Let him be placed in Perfect Buddhahood.

A: Let him be transfused as light
Into the Jewel-Ocean of the Unborn.
The time has come to leave this body
So heavy with blood, so bound with bones and veins.

B: Let him be placed in Perfect Buddhahood.

A: O Buddhas and Bodhisattvas, to catch him up with
your grace,

Catch him from the gulf of Karma,
From the red wind of the Bardo.

B: From the deceptions of the senses
From the blind angers of the animal body
From the blind pride of the forlorn ego
From the fearful heart's blind hold,
From the slavish mind's blind stupor
Let him be saved along the path
Along the bright light path of the Wisdom of Reality.
Now let him know his body nothing.

A: Let him escape forever the Wheel of Blood.

B: Let him be placed in Perfect Buddhahood.

Excerpt 2

SOLO: I see my people weeping
I see my family mourning
I see my body lying
What has happened to me? What has happened?

A: Turn your mind from the world, turn your mind to
recognise
The Shining Void of your true consciousness.
This is the first and greatest opening to Liberation:
This is Reality.

SOLO: They are stripping my body.
They are sweeping the place where I slept.

A: Recognise the Shining Void for your true consciousness:
This is Reality.

SOLO: I hear them calling for me. Do you hear me?
I am here. I am here. They ignore me.
What has happened to me? What has happened?

A: Let life go now, release it, do not
Cling to life in animal weakness, you may not –
However you cling you may not
Keep hold of the world.
Liberation opens: recognise it;
This is reality.

SOLO: What has happened to me? What has happened?

Excerpt 3
(*The terrifying visions must be seen as projections of his own mind.*)

A: Bound by evil Karma, bound by terror and longing,
    Resisting Grace, the five great Lights, the five wisdoms,
       you linger.
    These are illusory:
    These are your own mind:
    Had you recognised them
    Long since you had been gathered into a glorious
       Buddhahood.
B: Now you remain in the miseries of the Bardo.
C: (*Wail, as mourners.*)
SOLO: What new terrors? What new terrors?
    A furious dancing figure
    Burning with the five colours
    Brandishing a crescent blade
    Bringing a skull brimming blood
    Embraced by a red woman
    His right hand held high
    In the mudra of fascination.
    My heart begins to shake.
A: Nothing can come before you but the forms of your own
      mind.
SOLO: A figure out of the East
    White-hot, moon-white,
    Brandishing the skull
    That brims blood,
    Body coiled
    By a white woman
    And furiously dancing, furiously dancing,
    Smiling upon me:
    Strengthen me, strengthen me.
B: Do not fear them, do not fear them:
    Supplicate them, supplicate them.
SOLO: Out of the South
    A figure of flame
    Flame-yellow, a figure
    Flourishing a blade, balancing a skull

Brimming blood, and furiously dancing
Wrapped in the flame of a yellow Dakini,
Smiling upon me. Out of the West
A figure crimson
As the sun's core
Wound by a woman
Crimson as the sun's core
Furiously dancing.
Out of the North
A green figure,
Sword, skull, a scowling
Smile and the woman
And furiously dancing.

A: These are the Knowledge-holders:
These are from the Holy Paradise realms.
These come in compassion to receive you,
Each embraced by the Holy Mother.
Recognise them, supplicate them:
Here you may enter Paradise.

Excerpt 4

(*Solo describes the terrors encountered. He answers them as projections
of his own mind.*)

SOLO: Now my terrors begin, I have not yet tasted my terrors.
Baked blood-brown and triple-headed
With nine pitiless eyes forcing
Out of their sockets in fury, the eyebrows jerking,
Fangs of a tiger over his lips and
Grunting, whistling, gibbering, laughing,
Your feet rooted, yellow hair upright,
The three heads hung with human skulls and
Suns and moons and belly girdled
With skinned heads, with ebony serpents
Writhed in a garland. The first right hand
Grasping a wheel, and the next a skull-bowl,
The last a ploughshare. And a woman
Coils her body about him looping

Around his neck with her right hand and
Offering his lips a skull full of blood,
Fire spurts from their pores, their bodies
Rise like suns, on a dais of eagles:
Crackling, clashing, thundering.

A: Rising
Out of your own mind. Do not fear them.
These are your intellect embodied:
Buddha Heruka, the blood-drinker, rises
Embraced by Buddha Krotishaurima,
The Mother. Do not fear them. They are
In Reality Bhagavan Vairichana:
Recognise them: at that moment
Buddhahood shall receive you.

SOLO: My mind goes like a straw in the wind.
Strengthen me, strengthen me, O.

C: (*Wail, as mourners.*)

A: Miserable Karmic terror drives you ever deeper into the
Bardo.

SOLO: Others, others. Who are these others?

A & B: Recognise Vajra Meruka, the blood-drinker,
Recognise Vajra Krotishaurima,
Recognise Ratna Keruka, the blood-drinker,
Recognise Padma Krotishaurima,
Recognise Karma Heruka, the blood-drinker,
Recognise Karma Krotishaurima.

SOLO: I am blown like a breath through the Bardo.

A: Evil Karma drags you further, further and deeper into the
Bardo.

SOLO: I am blown like ashes through the Bardo.

B: Evil Karma catches you from yourself and from
Liberation.

A & B: Recognise these forms for your own mind.

SOLO: Filling the skies they crowd me away.

A: Evil Karma carries you away,
Darkens your eyes, fills you with terror, bears you deeper
into the Bardo.

Excerpt 5

SOLO: . . . without relief horrors assail me.
A white woman
Drinking blood
Out of a skull-bowl
Brandishing a human
Corpse as a club.
A woman of yellow,
The arrow at her ear,
The point on my heart.
A red woman, a black woman,
A red woman smiling upon me
Feeding herself with human entrails.
A dark-green woman
Stirring with a sceptre
A skullful of blood
And deliciously drinking.
And a whitish-yellow woman
Plucking a head off
And drinking the carcase.

A & B: Do not fear them. These shall teach you
Earthly existence: these are the forms
Of earthly existence, these are rising
Out of your mind and these await you.
Should your Karma return you to the Wheel of Blood.
Do not fear them, however they menace you.

SOLO: Strengthen me, O strengthen me.

A & B: O you Conquerors and you sons of Conquerors
Inhabiting the Ten Directions

SOLO: Inhabiting the Ten Directions

A & B: O you All-good Conquerors, the Peaceful and the Wrathful

SOLO: The Peaceful and the Wrathful

A & B: O you Gurus and Devas, and O you Dakinis, faithful ones

SOLO: O faithful ones

A & B: Turn in compassion towards him

SOLO: In compassion

A & B: Out of your great love strengthen him

C: (*Wail, as mourners.*)

SOLO: Strengthen me, strengthen me.
    Who are these? Rising to rend me,
    Lion-headed and blackish brown and shaking her mane and
        a corpse in her mouth,
    Tiger-headed and blood-coloured, the hands crossed
        downward, grinning against me,
    Baring her fangs and bulging her eyeballs;
    Fox-headed, black as carbon, a razor in her right hand,
        entrails in her left hand
    Entrails that she licks the blood from;
    Wolf-headed and blue as cobalt, rending a corpse and
        bulging her eyeballs;
    Vulture-headed and fang-yellow,
    Shouldering a giant corpse and shaking in her free hand a
        fleshless carcase.
A: These are the forms of your earthly existence.
SOLO: Headed like the cemetery bird and shouldering a gigantic
        corpse;
    Crow-headed, crow-coloured, holding a sword
    A skull-bowl and eating heart and lungs;
    Owl-headed and blue as starlight
    Carrying sceptre and skull-bowl and eating.
C1: Rend him, rend him, rend him, rend him.
C2: Slay, slay, slay, slay.
A: These are the eight Htamenmas, fear not.
    These are the thought-forms of earthly existence.
    Strengthen yourself: more fearful are rising.
SOLO: Brown yak-headed, yellowish red
    And snake-headed, greenish black
    And leopard-headed, monkey-headed,
    Red and snow-bear-headed, white
    And bear-headed, coming against me.
C1: Rend him, rend him, rend, rend.
C2: Slay, slay, slay, slay
A: These are the six yoginis out of your own brain's eastern
    quarter.
SOLO: Without relief, horrors assail me:
    Bat-headed, makara-headed,

Scorpion-headed, white kite-headed,
Fox-headed and tiger-headed.

A: These are the six yoginis out of your own brain's
southern quarter.

SOLO: Vulture-headed and horse-headed,
Eagle-headed and dog-headed,
Stag-headed and hoopoe-headed,
Wolf-headed and crow-headed,
Elephant-headed and snake-headed.

CI & C2: (*As before.*)

A & B: Nothing can come against you but the forms of your own
mind.
Fifty-eight blood-drinking deities now are risen against you.
The Deities of peace arose
From the voidness of the Dharma-Kaya.
These of wrath have risen
From the radiance of the Dharma-Kaya.
Know them for what they are, merging yourself
Into them in that knowledge: you will be gathered
Into Glorious Buddhahood in the same moment of time.

CI & C2: (*As before, crescendo.*)

SOLO: They fill up the vastness, their fangs
Bite down over their chins;
With eyeballs bulged and glaring,
Hair tied up on top of their heads
With pinched waists and swollen bellies,
Drinking blood, lapping up brains, rending corpses, filling
the worlds.

A: These are the thought-forms of earthly existence.

SOLO: Drinking blood, lapping up brains, rending corpses, filling
the worlds.

A & B: Know them for the radiance of the great Dharma-Kaya,
Be gathered into Buddhahood in the same moment of time.

CI & C2: (*As before.*)

SOLO: Terror drags me backward and downward.
Terror drags me by the hair
Backward and downward
Into darkness.

Excerpt 6
(*Urged to avoid rebirth.*)

SOLO: Am I to be plunged forever in the fleshly
  Anguish of an earthly existence?
  I am a being of evil Karma.
  I am a slave of evil Karma.

B: Evil Karma drives you to the doors of wombs.

SOLO: I see males and females: I see males embracing
    females.

B: Keep from between them: the womb opens between
    them.
  Regard them as our Guru and as the Divine Mother.
  Bow down before them,
  Worship with ardour,
  Exercise faith now,
  Closing the womb.

SOLO: The male stirs me to hatred but the female draws me in
    longing.

B: Abandon attraction and repulsion.
  Your evil Karma voraciously
  Hungers for rebirth. Resolve now, never
  To act upon attraction or repulsion:
  Hold your resolve,
  Closing the womb.

SOLO: Dazed as I am by evil Karma,
  Harried as I have been by the Bardo,
  The four elements in eruption
  And the unrelenting voices.

A: All your experience is but a mirage
  Mirrored or echoed.
  All your experience, all is unreal:
  Meditate this:
  Your lust or belief in their reality
  Will fade from you.
  What is to be gained lusting for attachment
  To these illusions?
  What advantage fleeing in terror
  From these illusions?

All is unreal:
Draw this teaching
Into your mind's
Inner continuum,
Closing the womb.

Homer

This is the only translation from Homer known to have been done by Ted Hughes. It was done for the sixth in 'a series of twelve programmes of verse translations from Homer, specially made by contemporary poets', read by Patrick Garland, and was transmitted on 10 November 1960 by the BBC Third Programme. Louis MacNeice and Anthony Thwaite, for the BBC Features Department, were responsible for this, with MacNeice dividing the epic into twelve parts and the poets being approached by Thwaite, who suggested to Hughes that he produce a version of 'The Storm', Book V, lines 382–493. Of others involved in the project, some knew Greek – e.g., Rex Warner, Peter Green, Alistair Elliot – while others, like Hughes, did not.

The proposal by Anthony Thwaite that Hughes contribute a translation of this particular passage fitted in well enough with the latter's preoccupations. His poem 'Everyman's Odyssey', which was first published in 1957 in a pamphlet, *Landmarks and Voyages*, and was subsequently included in *Lupercal* (1960), as well as his 1964 review of Mircea Eliade's *Shamanism*, testify to this.

Egbert Faas (*Ted Hughes: The Unaccommodated Universe*, 1980) quotes from the Eliade review, emphasising that for Hughes, as Hughes himself says, the shamanic flight was not a shaman monopoly but 'the basic experience of the poetic temperament'. He continues: 'It lies behind, e.g. the epic; of *Gilgamesh* and *Odysseus*. [. . .] It is the outline, in fact, of the Heroic Quest [. . .], one of the main regenerating dramas of the human psyche, the fundamental poetic event.' In a 1970 interview with Hughes, Faas queries Hughes on his being characterised as a poet of violence. Hughes responds: 'Who are the poets of violence? [. . .] [Y]ou'd have to begin with Homer, Aeschylus, Sophocles, Euripides, etc., author of Job, the various epics [. . .] [P]oetry is nothing if not [. . .] the record of just how the forces of the Universe try to redress some balance disturbed by human error.'

Later in the same interview, Faas asks about Hughes's interest in the *Bardo Thödol*, for which in 1960 Hughes had produced a libretto (see pp. 3–13). Hughes responds: '[T]he *Bardo Thödol* is basically a shamanistic flight and return. Tibetan Buddhism was enormously influenced by Tibetan primitive shamanism.' And as regards shamanism itself: 'The shaman's dream is the basis for the hero story. [. . .] it is the skeleton of thousands of folk tales and myths. And of many narrative poems, the *Odyssey*, the *Divine Comedy*, *Faust*, etc.'

The version printed here was first published in *Ted Hughes: Collected Poems* (Faber, 2003).

Odyssey: Book V, lines 350–450

And now Athene, daughter of Zeus, descended to change
    matters:
Reined back all blasts from their running and bound them
    in stillness.
Then called a smooth wind out of the North to flatten the
    mountainous water
Where the Zeus-born Odysseus laboured, and to help him
    to safety
With the Phaecians, those sea-farers.

Two nights and two days he floundered in massive seas
With the darkness of death breaking over and hollowing
    under.
Until, touched by the third dawn, all wind dropped of a
    sudden,
And in the airless after-calm
Craning around as the huge swell hoisted him upwards
He saw coast along the skyline. Then as children
See their father's life coming clear of the grip of an evil
That has stretched and drained him with agony long and
    binding,
And they rejoice that the gods have loosed him,
Odysseus exulted at his glimpse of the land and its trees,
And he drove through the waves to feel his feet upon
    earth.

But within hail of the land, heard sea rending on rock,
Eruption of the surge, whitening over the land-face,
Bundling everything in spray. No harbour fit for a ship and
    no inlet,
But thrust prows of crags and spines of reefs under hanging
    walls.

Then the heart of Odysseus shrank and he groaned:
'Against hope, Zeus gives this glance of the land,
And I have managed my body over the gulf
Only to find no way from the water. Offshore, horns of
　　rock,
Surf bellowing and mauling around them,
Behind them, empty cliff going up
And the sea crowding in deeply. Nowhere foothold
To step from disaster, but, in attempting,
A surge would uproot me and shatter me on rock-edges,
Sluicing my whole trouble to nothing. And if I swim on
　　further,
Seeking the sands of a bay where the sea goes in more
　　peaceably
Some squall will whirl down and drag me,
For all my protesting, out into depths and the maws of
　　ravenous fish,
Or a god fetch something monstrous up from the pit to
　　attack me –
One of the horde that feed at the hand of Amphitrite;
And I know too well how the Earth-shaker detests me.'

A mounding wave heaved him from his deliberations,
Building beneath him it carried and crashed him onto the
　　outworks.
There he would have been skinned in an instant
And the bones pestled within him,
But Owl-eyed Athene touched him. He plunged forward,
Both hands grasped rock, and he clung there groaning
As the mass ground over. So he survived it.
But, collapsing back, it stunned and tossed him far out into
　　the sea.
Thickly as gravel crusting the suckers
Of some octopus plucked from its crevice
The rock tore flesh from his fingers.
And there wretched Odysseus, buried in the backwash
　　welter,
Struggled with a death none had predicted
Till the Grey-eyed Athene found him.

Shouldering to air outside the surf and its wrack
He swam along watching the shore for a bay and quieter
  water.
Soon, off the mouth of a sweet river, saw landing,
Clear of rocks, and protected from the onset of open
  sea.
Feeling the shove of the current, he prayed in his heart to
  its god:
'Whoever you are, king, hear my prayers, for I come
Out of the sea's gape and Poseidon's anger.
The everlasting gods give ear to the prayer of a
  wanderer,
And a wanderer I come now, humbly to your waters,
After hard sufferings. Pity me, king, and take me into your
  care.'

Even as he spoke, the river stilled its momentum
And calming the chop of its waves and smoothing a path
Gathered the swimmer to safety. Now knees and thick arms
  folded:
His flesh swollen and his heart swamped by the seas
Odysseus slumped, unable to speak or move, and gulping
  at air
While sea-water belched from his mouth and nostrils.

Till his powers gathered and he stood. And unbinding the
  veil of the goddess,
Dropped it into the seaward river.
The weight of the current snatched it and in a moment Ino
  held it.
Then Odysseus turned from the river, kneeled in the reeds
  and kissing the earth
Groaned: 'What more misery now? And how shall a man
  get out of this?
What if I wait the night away, crouching here in the
  river-bottom?
Clamping frost and the saturating dews, sea-sodden as I am
  now,
Could be my death. And I know how bleakly
Wind before dawn comes off the water.

Or higher on the land, under the trees
And bedded in undergrowth, praying for the bone-chill
And fatigue to go from me, and praying for sleep to find me,
Maybe it will be the wild beasts that find me.'

Yet he took this last and climbed to a clump
Of trees in a clearing, near the water.
It was an olive and a wild olive knotting so densely one with
    the other

Neither the stroke of the naked sun
Nor wet sea-winds nor the needling rain could enter.
After his bitter ordeal, gladly royal Odysseus
Crept in under there and raked a bed wide
Where dead leaves were littered abundant enough
To warm two or three from the worst of winter.

Then he stretched out his body and heaped leaves over.
As one on a lonely farm and far from neighbours
Buries a live brand in black embers, preserving the seed
    of fire
Lest at need he be forced to go find fire elsewhere,
Odysseus hid under leaves. Then Athene ended his labours.
Covering his eyes, in sleep she released him.

Mário de Sá Carneiro

Born in Lisbon, Mário de Sá Carneiro (1890–1916) went to Paris in 1912, after a few months of half-hearted attendance at the Faculty of Law in Coimbra. He committed suicide in Paris. Sá Carneiro was the founder, and with Alvaro de Campos, alias Fernando Pessoa, the dominant literary personality of the magazine *Orpheu*. He is the author of short stories as well as poems.

Helder and Suzette Macedo collaborated with Ted Hughes on the translation of poems by Sá Carneiro, as well as poems by Helder Macedo himself. Letters from Hughes are illustrative of his scrupulously non-interventionist approach to the translation of poems by his contemporaries, even though he was concerned that he was being too free, and it is evident that he did take some 'liberties' (see Appendix 3). Noteworthy are his optimism and belief that given literal enough versions, he could be instrumental in producing something worth preserving, and that once this was done, the translations could not fail to find an interested readership. In a letter to Helder and Suzette Macedo, Hughes reiterated his belief in literal translation and his request for ad-verbum versions, or, as he called them, 'word by word transcriptions'.

Alcohol

Guillotines, battlements, bombardments
Winds far away in procession.
I am hurled through daffodil twilights
Bitten and purpled by some venom.

Winged haloes batter at my ears,
Griffins of stained odorous sound undulate around me,
Blades storm my eyesockets,
Havoc my soul and bleed out my senses . . .

In this loaded air I inhale myself.
I am of the light that lights me.
I want to pull myself together but go on disintegrating.
I fight, I enforce . . . useless! I float off . . .

I knot about my myself but am nowhere . . .
Everything heaves to foam that is crumbling
While a golden disc hurtles . . .
I close my eyes, the mist is terrifying . . .

What anaesthetic overpowers me now?
Opium of an underworld, not of an Eden.
How have I spellbound my own being?
What holy agony rarefies me?

Neither opium nor morphia flared through me –
Other alcohol, a slenderer stiletto . . .
Myself myself myself
So blinding a dawn, buried me in darkness.

'The two-faced, the pretender, with the lie in his marrow'

The two-faced, the pretender, with the lie in his marrow,
Who slid through his days from mask to mask,
The stucco King-moon, gaping in clownish amazement –
But under all that, the inching coward.

Not a courtier, a gatecrashing boor,
His soul of snow being the sick standing vapour of old
    vomit,
And the masterful heart he boomed for
A winded wheedling pansy.

No guts, no spur, an empty ninny
(With maybe a metronome under his ribs)
For all his yapping out of High Ideals

Sodden and venomous, and to be spat on,
This unfrocked wizard, this fat half-cat,
This balloon belching starry Empires.

'O fold me away between blankets'

O fold me away between blankets
And leave me alone.
And let the door of my room be locked forever –
Never to be opened, even for you, should you come.

Red wool and soft bed. Every chink definitely sealed.
Not a book by my bed – no, not one book.
Instead, at all times, there, just in reach,
Gorgeous patisseries and a bottle of Madeira.

Because I can't take any more. I don't even want toys.
What for? If I had them, I wouldn't know how to play.
What are they doing to me with their precautions and their
    attentions?
I'm not cut out for a fondling. Hands off! And leave me
    alone.

Let there be night in my room. The curtains always closed,
And I – tucked up neatly in my nest, all warm – what a
    darling!
Yes, to stay in bed forever, never to stir! To grow mouldy!
At least, it would be a complete rest . . . Nonsense! The best
    of lives.

If my feet hurt and I don't know how to walk straight
Why should I insist on going to parties, all dolled up like a
    lord?
Come, for once let my life go with my body
And resign itself to being hopeless . . .

Why should I go out if I catch cold unfailingly?
And who can I expect here, with my temperament?
Let your illusions go, Mario. Cosy eiderdown, cosy fire . . .
And forget the rest. This is enough, let's face it . . .

Let's give up. My longings will land me nowhere.
Why should I slog about in this imbecile crush?
Pity me! Help! For Christ's sake, take me to hospital . . .
That is, to a private ward: send the bill to my father.

That's the answer. A private ward, hygienic, spotless,
    modern and peaceful.
Preferably somewhere in Paris – it will make a better
    story –
In twenty years' time my poetry might get through,
And to be bats in Paris has a certain distinction, in the grand
    manner.

As for you, my love, you may come every Thursday,
If you want to be nice, and find how I am.
But you'll not set foot in my room, no, not in your sweetest
    mood –
Nothing doing, my pet. Baby's sleeping. All the rest is
    finished.

Helder Macedo

Helder Macedo, Camoëns Professor of Portuguese at King's College, London University, is a Fellow of the Academy of Sciences of Lisbon and former President of the International Association of Lusitanists (1993–99), as well as founder and editor of the journal *Portuguese Studies*. He is the author of five collections of poems. The following translation is included in a letter Hughes sent to Macedo. (See Appendix 4 for Suzette Macedo's literal version of the poem and for excerpts from letters from Suzette Macedo and from Hughes. Suzette Macedo notes that Hughes might well have preferred the author's literals, because they would probably have preserved the Portuguese syntax; she was aware that what Hughes evidently wanted was as direct, as unmediated a contact with the source text as possible.)

'When the mirror is broken open'

When the mirror is broken open
There is still the face
Precise and impersonal
To be unbound

When the mirror is broken open
Your nakedness and
Mine whisper
Together against us   (I mean conspiratorially)

When the mirror is broken open
My love
Let us search
So unendingly in each other we find

Where death forgets
Our deaths
Our hands
Holding torches   ('torches' isn't right)
                   'flames' might be better

Ferenc Juhász

Ferenc Juhász was born into a peasant family in western Hungary in 1928. His earliest collections appeared in 1949 and 1950. In 1954 he published an epic poem, *Prodigal Land*, about Dozsa, the martyr leader of the 1514 peasant rebellion. Juhász is a prolific poet, much of his work originating in a folk-tale peasant tradition.

Hughes had seen Juhász's long poem 'The Boy Changed into a Stag Cries Out at the Gate of Secrets' in an anthology, *The Plough and the Pen: Writings from Hungary 1930–1956*, edited by Ilona Duczynak and Karl Polanyi, with an introduction by W. H. Auden (1963). Like Auden himself, who calls the poem 'one of the greatest poems written in my time', Hughes was enormously impressed, although the translation, by Kenneth McRobbie, seemed to him problematical. One might ask how he could judge, since he could not read the Hungarian original; the answer, which might not satisfy everybody, has to be that he sensed it. While I was visiting him in Devon to plan an issue of *Modern Poetry in Translation* which he hoped to devote to contemporary Hungarian poetry, Hughes rewrote the Juhász translation, working with great concentration and at speed. I carried it off with me, but as the issue for which it was intended was indefinitely postponed, I returned it to the author. I fortunately found it again in Special Collections in the Robert W. Woodruff Library, Emory University, Atlanta, and it was published with a brief introduction in *Modern Poetry in Translation*, New Series, No. 21, 2003.

'What is intriguing', as I wrote elsewhere (*Letters to Ted*, Anvil, 2002), 'is that [Hughes] felt able to rewrite the English version without reference to any source text. It is interesting that he is able, in this situation, simply to write his own version, based on someone else's, whereas in other circumstances, e.g., when faced by the poet himself or by the source text in a literal translation, he feels compelled to stay as close as possible to the wording and even syntax of the original.'

I have corrected some obvious typos. Where Hughes has written an alternative word in the margin and deleted the original, I have altered the text accordingly. Where he has not deleted the original I have included both words. The lineation appears not to have been finalised and I have left it as is. I have, however, somewhat regularised the punctuation.

Appendix 5 includes versions by Kenneth McRobbie and David Wevill of the opening lines of the poem. (For the full Wevill text, see *Selected Poems of Sándor Weöres and Ferenc Juhász*, Penguin, 1970, Weöres's poetry being translated by Edwin Morgan.)

The Boy Changed into a Stag Cries Out at the Gate of Secrets

The mother called after her son
from the far distance
The mother called after her son
from the far distance,
she went out in front of the house, calling
and she loosened her hair's thick knot
which the dusk wove to a dense, stirring veil,
a valuable robe sweeping the earth,
wove to a stiff and heavily-flaring mantle,
a banner for the wind with ten black tassels,
a shroud, in the fire-slashed blood-heavy twilight.
She twisted her fingers among the fine tendrils
of the stars, the moon's suds bleached her features,
and she called after her son shrilly
as she called him long ago, a small child,
she went out from the house talking to the wind,
and spoke to the song-birds, her words overtaking
the wild geese going in couples,
to the shivering bullrushes,
to the potato flower in its pallor,
to the clench-balled bulls rooted so deeply,
to the fragrant shadowy sumch, [mulch?]
she spoke to the fish where they leaped playfully,
to the momentary oil-rings, mauve and fleeting.
    You birds and branches, hear me,
listen as I cry,
    listen, you fishes and you flowers,
listen, I cry to be heard,
    listen, you glands of the pumping soils,
    you vibrant fins, you astral-seeding parachutes,

decelerate, you humming motors of the saps,
screw down the whining taps in the depth of the atom,
    all iron-pelvissed virgins,
    sheep alive under cotton,
listen as I cry,
I am crying out to my son.

The mother called out to her son
and her cry climbed in a spiral
within the gyre of the cosmos it ascended,
her limbs glancing in the lightrays
like the skid-scaled flanks of a fish,
or a roadside boil of salt or crystal.
The mother called out to her son,
    Come back, my own son, come back,
      I am calling, your calm harbour,
    Come back my own son, come back,
      I am calling, your pure fountain,
    Come back, my own son, come back,
      I am calling, the breast where your memory sucked,
    Come back, my own son, come back,
      I am calling, your almost sightless lamp.
Come back, my own son, for this world of spiky objects has
    put out my eyes,
my eyes are sealed under yellow-green bruises, my jaw
    contracts,
my thighs and my shins are skinned,
from every side things batter in on me like crazed rams,
the gate, the post, the chair try their horns on me,
doors slam against me like drunken brawlers,
the vicious electricity snaps at me,
my scaling skin leaks blood,
a bird's beak crushed with a rock,
scissors slither off like spider-crabs of nickel,
the matches are sparrowfeet, the pail hacks back at me with
    its handle.

Come back, my own son, come back,
my legs no longer lift me like the young hind,
    festering blooms open on my feet,

gnarled tubers screw into my purpling thighs,
the skin over my toes glazes to bone,
    my fingers harden, already the flaking flesh
shells off like slate from weathered geologic formations,
    every limb has served its time and sickens.

Come back, my own son, come back
    for I am no longer as I was,
    I am a used-up shadow from the inner visions
    that flare through the thickening organs
    like an old cock's crowing, on winter dawns,
from a fence of shirts hanging board-frozen.
I am calling, your own mother,
come back, my own son, come back,
force new order onto the anarchic things,
discipline the savage objects, tame the knife and domesticate
    the comb,
because now I am only two gritty green eyes
glassy and weightless, like the dragonfly,
whose winged nape and mouth, that you know so well, so
    delicately clasp
two crystal apples in the green-illumined skull,
I am two staring eyes without a face,
seeing all, and one with the unearthly beings.
Come back, my own son, come back into place,
    with your fresh breath bring everything again to
    order/into place.

In the remote forest the boy heard.
He jerked up his head in an instant,
his spread nostrils testing the air,
his soft dewlap throbbing, the veined ears pointing
tautly to that lamenting music
as to the still tread of the hunter,
as to hot wisps fronding from the cradle
of a forest fire, when the skyline trees
smoke and begin to whimper bluely.
He turned his head to the old voice,
and now an agony fastens on him,
and he sees the shag hair over his buttocks,

and he sees, on his bony legs,
the cleft hooves that deal his track,
sees, where lilies look up in pools,
low-slung hair-pursed buck-balls.
He forces his way towards the lake,
crashing the brittle willow thickets,
haunches plastered with foam that spatters
to/on the earth at his every bound,
his four black hooves rip him a path
through a slaughter of wild flowers,
sock a lizard into the mud,
throat ballooned and tail sheared,
till he reaches the lake at last,
and looks in at its lit window
that holds the moon, moving beech-boughs,
and a stag staring at him.
For the first time he sees the bristling pelt
covering all his lean body,
hair over knees and thighs, the transverse
tasselled lips of his male purse,
his long skull treed with antlers,
bone boughs bursting to bone leaves,
his face closely furred to the chin,
his nostrils slit and slanted in.
The great antlers knock against trees,
roped veins lump on his neck,
he strains fiercely, stamping he tries
to put out an answering cry, but in vain,
it is only a stag's voice belling
in the throat of this mother's son,
and he scatters a son's tears, trampling the shallows
to drive out that lake-horror, scare it
down into the whirlpool gullet
of the water-dark, where glittering
little fishes flicker their laces,
miniature bubble-eyed jewellery.
The ripples smooth off into the gloom,
but still a stag stands in the foam of the moon.

Now in his turn the boy cries back,
   stretching up his bellowing neck,
Now in his turn the boy cries back
   crying through fog from a stag's throat,
      Mother, my mother
      I cannot come back.
      Mother, my mother
      you must not lure me,
      mother, my mother,
      my maker, my nurse,
      mother, my mother
      fresh foaming/bubbling fountain,
      safe arms that held me,
      big breasts that fed me,
      my tent in the frost,
      mother, my mother,
      never seek my coming
      mother, my mother
      my frail silky stem,
      mother, my mother,
      my gold-mouthed bird
      mother, my mother
      you must not lure me.
      If I should return
      my horns would split you,
      from point onto point/fork onto fork
      tossing your body,
      if I should return
      you would fall under me,
      your loose veiny breasts
      shredded by hooves,
      I'd stab with bare tines,
      I'd rip with my teeth,
      and stamp in your womb, even,
      if I should return
      I'd hook your lungs from you,
      blue flies would be clouding,
      stars would gaze
      on your spilled flower-vitals,

which once housed me,
they were summer suns over me,
a glistening peace
their warm clasp unbroken
as once the warm cattle
breathed gently to Jesus.
Mother, my mother
do not summon me,
your death would be home
as my shape entered,
as this son approached you.
Every prong of my antlers
is a golden thread,
every branch of my antlers
a winged candelabra,
each spine of my antlers
a catafalque candle,
each leaf of my antlers
a gold-laced altar.
It would be your death
to see my grey antlers
lifting in the sky
like an All Souls
candlelit cemetery,
my head a stone tree
and the leaves flames lengthening.
Mother, my mother,
if I came near you,
I would burn you like tinder grass,
scorch you to charred clay,
you'd explode like resin,
and I would roast you
to black rags of flesh.
Mother, my mother
do not summon me,
I would devour you
at my coming,
your bed would be havoc,
your flower garden

ploughed by the thousand
blades of my antlers.
I'd chew through the trees
in the stag-torn coppice,
empty the one well
with one swallowing,
at my coming
your cottage would be blazing,
then I would run
to the ancient graveyard,
with my narrow soft nose
with my four hooves
I'd dig up my father,
my teeth would be wrenching
the cracked coffin lid
to scatter the bones.
Mother, O mother
do not lure me,
I cannot come back,
if I come back
I bring your death.

In a stag's voice the boy cried,
And in these words his mother answered:
    Come back, my son, come back,
I call you, your own mother,
    come back, my own son, come back,
I'll cook brown broth and into it you'll slice onion rings.
They'll crunch in your bite like quartz splintering in the
    champ of a giant,
I'll bring you warm milk in a jug
and trickle wine from my last keg into bottles necked like
    the heron,
and I know how to knead bread under my stony knuckles, I
    know how you like it,
bread to bake to soft-bellied buns, the sweet bread for feasts,
    come back, my own son, come back.
From the live breasts of screeching geese I have pulled the
    down for your eiderdown,

weeping I plucked my weeping geese, and the bald
   patches whitened angrily on their breasts, like the mouths
      of the dying,
I have shaken out your mattress in the sun, freshened it for
   your sleeping
the yard is swept for your coming, the table is laid.

Mother, my mother,
   for me there'll be no homecoming
do not lay the plaited white bread out for me,
   or the goat's sweet milk foaming in my flowered mug
do not prepare my soft bed for me,
   or ravage the breasts of the geese for their feathers,
pour away your wine, let it soak into my father's grave,
   braid the lovely onions in a garland,
fry up for the little ones the big-bellied frothy-topped
   dough.

The milk would be vinegar at a touch of my tongue
and the white bread would be struck to a stone turtle
your wine filling/spilling like warm blood into my
   tumbler
the eiderdown dissolving in a silence of blue flame
and the brittle-beaked mug splintered to swordgrass.

O mother, O mother, my own good mother,
   my step will never ring out in my father's house,
I have to live in the thick of the forest,
   your shadowed house has no room for my meshed
      antlers
Your yard has no room for my cemetery antlers
   because my reaching-out horns are a loud world tree,
their foliage arches to constellations, their green moss
   is the Milky Way,

Into my mouth comes only sweet-breathed herbs,
only the first-growth grasses that melt my saliva
and I can never drink again from the flowered mug you
   bring me,
only from a clear brook, only from a clear brook.

I do not understand, I do not understand your strange and
    tormented words, my son,
you speak like a stag, a stag's spirit has possessed you, my
    unhappy one.
When the turtledove cries, when the turtledove cries, when
    the little bird sings, when the little bird sings, my son,
why in the whole Universe am I the last soul left, the
    solitary one?
Do you remember, do you remember, your small once-young
    mother, my son?
I do not understand, I do not understand your sad and
    tortured words, O my long-lost son.
Do you remember how you came running, running home to
    me, so happy with your school report,
you dissected a bull-frog, splayed his freckled paddle feet
    on the fence,
how you pored over books about aircraft and followed me
    in to help with the washing,
you loved Irene B, your friends were VJ and HS, the wild
    and orchid-bearded painter,
and do you remember the Saturday nights, when your father
    came back sober how happy you were?

O mother, my mother, do not speak of my sweetheart of
    those days, or of my friends,
they flit by like fish in the cold depths, that painter with
    his chin of vermilion
who knows down what road he has gone shouting, who
    knows, mother, where my boyhood has gone?
Mother, my mother, do not remember my father, for sorrow
    has bloomed from his flesh,
sorrow flowers out of the dark earth, do not remember my
    father, my father,
he'll heave from the earth, gathering about him his
    yellowing bones,
and stagger from the grave with his nails and his hair new-
    grown.
Oh, oh, Uncle Wilhelm came, the coffin maker with his
    puppet mask,

He told us to hold your feet and drop you neatly into the coffin,
And I retched because I was frightened. I had come that day
        from Pest,
    you too, my father, went back and forth to Pest, an office
        messenger, till the rails writhed up,
    such rending knives in my belly then, your tight cheeks
        gashed by the candle's shadows.
Your new son-in-law, Lacy the barber, shaved you with care,
        while the candle dribbled like a silent baby,
    regurgitating its glistening entrails, its long luminous
        nerves like vines,
    the choral society surrounded you under their purple hats,
        mourning you at the tops of their voices,
    with one finger tip I traced the rim of your forehead, your
        hair was so alive,
I heard it growing, I saw the bristles thicken and your chin
        blackened by morning, and the next day your throat
    sunken
        in under spines of new hair like the snake-grass,
    curved like a soft-haired cantaloupe, cabbage skin blue
        under the yellow hair of the caterpillar,
Oh and I thought your hair, your beard, would bush the
        whole room full, and would overgrow the yard
    and the entire world, that the stars would nestle like cells
        in the living strands.
Ah the ponderous green rain began to fall then, and the team
        of red horses on the hearse whinnied in terror,
    one lashing out over your head with a thunderbolt hoof, the
        other relentlessly pissing,
    so that his purple parts passed out with it like a hanged
        man's tongue, while the coachman cursed.
The downpour sluiced around the huddled brassbandsmen,
        and then all those old friends blew with a will
    blew as they wept, by the chapel wall studded with
        globe thistles,
    the old friends blew till their lips swelled purple and the
        music spiralled out and up,
    the old friends blew till their lips cracked, till their lips
        bled, their eyeballs staring,

blew for the cards and the booze, and the trumped women,
    the bloated and the withered,
blew for the beer-money of their redletter days, the tips
    tossed whirling into space after you,
blew as they sobbed, blew sadly down into sedimentary
    layers of silted sadness,
music poured from the burnished mouths, from rings of
    brass into putrefying nothingness,
out of it streamed the petrified sweethearts, rotten women
    and mouldered grandfathers, out of the music,
with little cottages, cradles and a whole generation of
    silver-bellied watches thick with enamel, rolling like
    onions,
Easter bells and multitudinous Saviours flew out on the wide
    spread wings of the sound,
with railway wheels and infantrymen brass-buttoned at the
    salute, and satchels,
the old friends played on, teeth crimsoning under lips that
    peeled back swelling like blackened liver,
and yourself conducting the choir: well done boys, that's
    grand, don't stop now, keep it up,
all the time your hands folded hard, and those gold spiders
    with their huge wheel-spoke-jointed legs sitting on
    your heart,
and in the cupboard your collapsed boots wait for their
    relatives, the white socks on your curling bread
    crust feet,
the old friends blew for you that day out under the crashing
    rain, valves snapping like Adam's apples of steel,
fangs of antediluvian birds, teeth of the Carchoradon,
    crusing for carrion out of the brazen mouths of
    the trumpets,
O mother, my mother, do not recall my father,
let my father lie, lest his eyes erupt from suddenly opening
    earth.

    The mother called after her son
    from the far distance,
    come back, my own son, come back,

turn from that stone world,
you stag of the stone forest, the chemical air, the
    electric grids,
industrial lightning, riveted bridges, streetcars, lap
    at your blood,
hourly they attack you a hundred times afresh, yet you
    never hit back,
I am calling, your own mother,
    come back, my own son, come back.

He stood on the perpetually renewing crags of time,
he stood over the Universe, on the ringed summit,
there the boy stood at the gate of secrets,
his stag's antlers were toying with the stars,
and his stag's voice down the lost paths of the world
    answered to his mother his maker

    Mother, my mother, I cannot come back,
new gold boils in my hundred wounds,
every day a hundred bullets blast me off my feet,
every day, get up a hundred times more whole,
every day I die three billion times,
every day I am born three billion times,
every branch of my antlers is a double-based pylon,
every tine of my antlers is a high-tension cable
my eyes are ports for sea-going tankers, my veins are
    tarry hawsers, my teeth
are iron bridges, in my heart surge the monster-infested
    seas,
each vertebra is a seething capital, and a barge belching
    black smoke is my spleen,
my every cell is a factory, my every atom a solar system,
and sun and moon swing in my testicles,
and the Milky Way is in my bone marrow,
space's every point is a part of my body,
and my brain's rhythms come in from far out in the
    circling galaxies.

O my lost son, no matter for that,
    your mother's eyes are sleepless, they watch for
      you still.

Only to die shall I come back, only to die shall I come back,
yes, shall come back to die
and when I have come, but only to die, O my mother,
then you can stretch me out in my father's house,
then with your marble hands you can wash my body,
then you can close my glandulous eyelids with a kiss,
    and then when my flesh falls to pieces
and lies in its stench, yet deep among flowers,
    then I shall feed on your blood and be fruit of your body
then I shall be your own small son once more,
and this shall give pain to you alone, O mother,
to you alone, O my mother.

Yves Bonnefoy

Yves Bonnefoy, leading French poet, essayist, translator and art historian, was born in 1923. He moved to Paris in 1944, where he took a degree in philosophy, also studying mathematics and philosophy at the University of Poitiers. In Paris Bonnefoy became closely associated with the Surrealist circle, and under its influence published his first literary work, *Traité du pianiste* (1946). His first important collection of poems, *Du Mouvement et de l'immobilité de Douve*, from which Hughes made his own selection, gained critical acclaim. *Hier régnant désert* (1958), his second collection of poems, received the Prix de l'Express. In 1967, with others, Bonnefoy founded *L'éphemère*, a journal of art and literature, now defunct. Since the 1960s he has published several works on art and art history. Bonnefoy has travelled widely, and taught literature at a number of universities in the US and Europe. He has received many awards. Besides his much admired translations of a dozen plays by Shakespeare, he has translated a number of poets, including Donne, Keats, Leopardi and Yeats. In 1981 he was elected to the Collège de France after the death of Roland Barthes, the first poet to hold a chair since Paul Valéry.

Below are some excerpts from a note written by Anthony Rudolf, Yves Bonnefoy's principal British translator, for *Modern Poetry in Translation* (New Series, No. 21), which also featured Hughes's translation of the long Ferenc Juhász poem (see pp. 25–37). Hughes's draft translations from Bonnefoy's *Du Mouvement et de l'immobilité de Douve* were transcribed by Rudolf from the notebooks. Appended are some additional notes prepared by Anthony Rudolf.

[. . .] Ted Hughes was the founder of Poetry International [in London], which first took place in 1967. Yves Bonnefoy was one of the participants invited to that gathering of famous poets. I had already been translating Bonnefoy for about four years. It was my friend Alberto de Lacerda who brought my translations to the attention of Nathaniel Tarn, and it was certainly Tarn [translator of Neruda and an early advisory editor of *Modern Poetry in Translation*] who brought them to the attention of Ted Hughes.

I learned that Hughes himself would be one of the readers of translations alongside the original poets. I am inclined to think that Ted Hughes started translating Bonnefoy for Poetry International, perhaps because he did not know of any other versions and then, doubtless having other priorities, ceded to me when he learned of my translations. [. . .] Another possibility

[. . .] is that Hughes translated the poems for private reasons, in order to get to know them better. Whichever explanation is the correct one and even allowing for the fact that these versions are a first draft, the hard-line literality of some solutions raises fascinating questions about Hughes's approach to poetry translation. It is evident from an unsigned *MPT* editorial that Hughes had already embarked on his strategy of rough/literal versions [. . .]

Even the first draft of a version by one great poet of another will be of abiding interest [. . .]. There are brilliant local victories among the failures and mistakes in this first draft, but we will never know, and more's the pity, what Ted Hughes would have ended up with. He and I sometimes discussed Bonnefoy, but he never referred to his own version. [. . .] Yves Bonnefoy himself, who met Ted Hughes for the first and only time at that Poetry International, is moved and fascinated by this discovery among Hughes's manuscripts.

Three

It marked itself with a wind stronger than our memories,
Stupor of robes and cry of stones – and you passed before
    the flames
With head quartered and hands riven and all
In quest of death on the exultant drums of your gestures
    (heroic deeds).

It was day of your breasts
And at last you reigned outside my head (absent from my
    head).

Four

I awake, it is raining. The wind penetrates you, Douve,
    resinous waste lulled asleep close to me. I am on a terrace,
    in a hole of death. Great dogs of foliage tremble.

The arm you hold up, suddenly, in a doorway (gorge),
    blazes
the ages alight. Village of embers, every moment I see you
    born, Douve,

Every moment die.

Six

What pallor strikes you, underground river, what artery
    bursts in you, where the echo of your fall resounds?

This arm you heave up suddenly opens, bursts into flame.
    Your face recoils. What growing fog tears your core from
    me? Slow cliff of shadow, frontier of death.

Mute arms gather you, trees of another shore.

Seven

Confused wounded in the leaves,
But carried off by the blood of footprints that lose
    themselves,
Accomplice of life still.

I have seen you sand-spattered at the end of your struggle
Hesitate at the borders of silence and of water,
And the soiled mouth of the last stars
Break with a cry of horror from aging in your night.

O raising in the hard air sudden as a rock
A beautiful gesture of coal.

Eight

The ridiculous music begins in the hands, in the knees, then
it is the head which crackles, the music affirms itself under
    the lips. Its certitude penetrates the versant (pouring,
    overturning) of the face.

Just now dislocating the facial carpentry. Just now one
    proceeds to the uprooting of the view.

Twelve

I see Douve stretched out. In the scarlet village of the air,
where the branches fight on her face, where roots search
their paths through her body – she radiates a strident joy
of insects, a fearful music.

At the black step of the earth, Douve ravaged, exultant,
rejoins the knotty lamp of the plateaux.

Fifteen

O endowed with a profile where the earth fleshes its frenzy,
I see you vanish.

The naked earth on your lips and the shiver of the silex
Invent your last smile,

Profound science where the ancient
Cerebral bestiary calcines itself.

Seventeen

The gulley penetrates your mouth now,
The five fingers deploy themselves in the fortunes of the
forest now,
The first head flows between the grasses now,
The throat paints itself with snow and wolves now,
The eyes *wind* on what fleetings of death and it is us in this
wind in this water in this cold now.

NOTES

[by Anthony Rudolf]

'Three' – *marked*. This is a guess – completely illegible. Perhaps TH misread
'il s'agissait' as 'il s'agitait'.
gestures (heroic deeds). The phrase in parenthesis is TH's alternative version,
suggestive of dictionary research or his own knowledge, but either way it
should have been rejected.

absent from my head. The phrase in parenthesis is TH's alternative version.

'Four' – *gorge*. The word in parenthesis is TH's alternative version, suggestive of dictionary research, but in this sense 'porte' is usually plural, which TH has not noticed, and this alternative should have been rejected; it was clearly suggested by the first paragraph of this poem.

'Six' – *growing*. The word is fairly illegible but 'growing' makes sense of the French word 'croissant'.
core. The word could be either 'core' or 'love' but both are strange and surely un-Hughesian extrapolations from the meanings of the French word 'regard'. A stretch of the retinal imagination could detect the correct word 'look' in his handwriting.

'Seven' – *last*. Likeliest reading of illegible word.
aging. TH evidently has confused 'vieillir', 'to age' with 'veiller', 'to watch'.

'Eight' – *versant (pouring, overturning)*. TH's parenthetical proposals suggest that he did not have his dictionary to hand at this point, since the French word 'versant' = 'slope'. And yet, had he not guessed at it – presumably from his knowledge of the meaning of the verb 'verser' – he could have left the archaic English word 'versant' (or slope) as it was.

'Twelve' – *village*. TH has misread 'ville' (city) as 'village'.

'Fifteen' – *fleshes*. If this smudged and virtually illegible word is 'fleshes', one wonders how TH arrived at 'fleshes its frenzy'. Perhaps an association with 'charnel'? 'S'acharner' means 'persist'.

'Seventeen' – *first head*. The French 'tête première' means 'primal head'.
wind. This is a rather Poundian translation of 'ventent'. It should, of course, be 'blow'.

Paul Eluard

From 1919 to 1938, Paul Eluard (1895–1952) was a leading member of the Surrealist movement, exploring dreams, the unconscious and mental alienation. In the 1930s he broke with Surrealism, and in 1942 joined the Communist Party. Eluard was one of the most celebrated of the Resistance writers. He remained a committed Communist until his death.

Hughes's draft translations of poems by Eluard are in manuscript, in notebooks, and in letters to his sister, Olwyn. They are quite painstakingly transcribed, suggesting that there may have been earlier drafts. Some of the translations in Hughes's handwriting were deciphered by Olwyn Hughes, others by Daniel Weissbort and Professor Norma Rinsler, some of whose comments are included below. The same notebook contains as well two draft translations of poems by Baudelaire.

The selection is mostly from Paul Eluard, *Choix de poèmes* (Gallimard, three editions). The French title is included below and the source texts may be found either in *Choix de poèmes* or in the Pléiade edition of Eluard's complete works.

Although one can see why Hughes might have been interested in Eluard, it remains uncertain why he should have produced quite so many versions (forty). Olwyn Hughes recalls that she sent Hughes a volume of Eluard in the late 1950s, at a time when he was in the US. French was the only foreign language he could work with directly, and it is clear that these translations, which perhaps he undertook initially as a diversion, were no more than drafts. Nevertheless, the selection itself is of interest and many of the literal versions are lucid and forceful. Eluard's importance for Hughes at this time can be gleaned from his comment in a letter to Olwyn Hughes (1961): 'He's done me a tremendous amount of good – really shown me how to get beyond my last stage, at which I was a bit stuck and shown me how to shake off the English trotting harness in which every single poet in England performs.' Elsewhere, he writes: 'Eluard is just what I need. I'm much too objective and matter of fact to be melted down by him, but he does encourage my own fluencies. His absolutely musical way of building a poem up is something the stupid good manners and scissor-fencing of English modern poetry doesn't permit among its precieuses.'

There was also a practical reason for Hughes to work on Eluard to the extent that he did, namely the likelihood of publication in the Penguin Modern

European Poets series that was edited by Nikos Stangos. Hughes wrote to Olwyn Hughes: 'I have had a chance to translate Eluard for Penguin. I'm a bit reluctant to start on this translating lark, but I find it very easy to make quite close versions, quite good poetry, and if I had someone to check my French it might be worth it. [. . .] I've read most of the CHOIX now, and roughly translated many of them [. . .].'

Hughes confirmed this interest in another letter to Olwyn Hughes (from Devon): 'I'm now thinking quite seriously of doing a translation of about 60 poems of Eluard, and now I have time and space it shouldn't take long. I'll enclose a few rough attempts with the play [he was probably alluding here to *Ondine*, an early play by Jean Giraudoux]. Could you send me the odd French literary magazine? [. . .] Whatever you think might interest me in the magazine line, or French poetry; please send it, since I want to qualify my sense of belonging to the English mentality as much as possible, and I would prefer to be mostly aware of any other capital's literary life than London's. Thank God it seems so dim and far a place.'

Interesting, of course, is the importance he ascribed to involvement, via translation, in another literature. As Olwyn Hughes points out, it is arguable that Eluard opened for Ted Hughes the door to European poetry in general. He was wholly dependent on others, János Csokits for instance in translating János Pilinszky's poetry, and the author himself in translating Yehuda Amichai's. In both these cases, while he did not translate directly from the source-language texts, he had the benefit of an unusually close living connection with them. His insistence on literalism had to do with the obligation he felt to remain as verbally close as possible to the source texts.

Cow [Vache]

> Nobody leads the cow
> To the greenery cropped and dry
> To the greenery without caresses.
>
> The grass which receives it
> Must be sweet as a silken thread,
> A thread of silk sweet as a thread of milk.
>
> Ignored mother
> For the children it is not lunch,
> But the milk on the grass.

The grass before the cow,
The child before the grass.

Fish [Poisson]

The fish, the bathers, the boats
Transform the water.
The water is gentle it stirs
Only for what touches it.

The fish advances
Like a finger in a glove,
The bather dances slowly
And the sail breathes.

But the soft water moves
For whatever touches it
For the fish, for the bather, for the boat
That it carries
(And) that it carries away.

Wet [Mouillé]

The stone bounces on the water,
Smoke cannot enter there.
Water, such a skin
That nothing can wound it,
Is caressed
By man and by fish.
Chirrupping* like a bowstring
The fish, when a man catches it,
Dies, unable to swallow
This planet of air and light.

And the man sinks to the bottom of water
For the fish

* The source text's '*claquant*' is also slang for 'to die'. Perhaps Eluard was thinking of the fish's tail drumming on the ground? [NR]

Or for the bitter solitude
Of water supple and always closed.

'The hairless gluttony' [Quatres Gosses]

The hairless gluttony,
Swelling his cheeks,
Swallowing a flower,
Fragrant skin interior.
Wise child,
Whistle,
Mouth forcefully red
Light mouth under the ponderous head
One to ten, ten to one
The orphan,
The breast that nourished him covered with black
Will not wash him.
Foul
Like a night-forest in winter.
Dead,
The [illegible. Fr: *belles*] teeth, but the lovely eyes immobile.
Set.
What fly of his life
Was the mother of the flies of his death.

'You rise the water opens' [Tu te lèves l'eau se déplie]

You rise the water opens
You lie down the water spreads,

You are water turned back from its gulfs
You are the earth that takes root
And on which all things are established

You make bubbles of silence in the desert of uproars
You sing night hymns on the cords of the rainbow
You are everywhere you cancel all roads

You sacrifice time
To the eternal youth of the exact flame
That robs nature in reproducing it

Woman you put to the world a body always like
Yours

You are resemblance

'At the first clear word' [Au premier mot limpide]

At the first clear word
at the first laugh of your flesh
The thick* road vanishes
Everything starts afresh

The timid flowers the flowers without air of the night sky
Hands veiled with clumsiness
Child's hands

Eyes raised toward your face & it is day on earth
The first youth ends [ended/closed etc?]†
The sole pleasure

Hearth of earth hearth of perfumes and of dew
Without age without reasons without bond,
Forgetfulness without shade.

In the Virgin Mountain [Dans la montagne vierge]

The grasses and the flowers do not abandon me
Their scent follows the wind

The kids play in that youth
An eagle makes a full-stop in the heaven without secrets

---

* Thick/*épais* is difficult! It does mean 'thick', but the translation depends on context. I see the road as running between bushes on both sides, so that you have to fight your way through.
† Should be present tense: vanishes; starts.

The sun is living his feet are on the earth
Its colours make the blushing cheeks of love
And the [illegible. Fr: *humaine*] human light dilates with
    ease.

Man in greatness at the heart of an imperishable world
Inscribes his shadow on the heaven and his fire on the earth.

Mount Grammos [Le mont Grammos]

Mount Grammos is a bit rough
But men soften it

The savages we kill them
We shorten our night

More brutes than cannon powder
Our enemies ignore us

They know nothing of man
Nor of his arrant power

Our heart polishes the stone.

Old Youth [Vieille jeunesse]

At the fountain he gives her a kiss on the mouth
Under the empty sky he gave her his ten fingers and his eyes
In time he gave her his life and his children

The faithful echo repeated without end this song
The clear mirror of the human body makes of it all a
    banquet
A way of living a way of being and the unique right
Of defending himself without doubting his eternity.

Yehuda Amichai

Yehuda Amichai (1924–2000) was born in Würzburg, Germany, into an orthodox Jewish family, and emigrated to Palestine in 1936. He served with the Jewish Brigade in the British Army during World War II, and as an infantryman in the Palmach, the elite strike force, in the Israeli War of Independence, as well as in two other Israeli wars (1956 and 1973). He studied Hebrew literature and the Bible at the Hebrew University, and he taught these subjects in teachers' seminars at the Hebrew University school for foreign students. Amichai frequently visited the US as a visiting poet and lecturer. He was honoured nationally and internationally, being a recipient of the Israeli Shlonsky, Brener, Bialik and Acum prizes and others. He had honorary degrees from the Hebrew University, Tel Aviv University, the Hebrew Union College and the Weitzman Institute, and was a Distinguished Associate Fellow of the American Academy for the Arts and Sciences. Amichai published many collections of poetry in Hebrew and more collections in English translation, probably, than any other contemporary non-English poet. He also published fiction and plays.

Amichai gave readings in many countries, including the UK, for instance at the first Poetry International in London, directed by Ted Hughes, in 1967. Ted Hughes collaborated with him on three collections: *Selected Poems* (1968; with Assia Gutmann), *Amen* (1978) and *Time* (1979), the latter two translated with Amichai himself. In the last year of his life, Hughes and the present writer collaborated on a selection of 'the best' of Amichai's poetry in English translation (Faber, 2000).

It has become apparent that Amichai's was a distinctly modern literary enterprise, both in content and in language; as he put it in 'National Thoughts' (see below), 'The language which described God and the Miracles, / Says: / Motor car, bomb, God.' He draws from diverse historical stages of the language, from classical or Biblical Hebrew, through that of the Spanish Golden Age (see 'Ibn Gabirol', below; Hughes attempted, with Assia Gutmann, to translate some poems by Solomon Ibn Gabirol, 1021/22–*c*.1055, one of the greatest Hebrew lyric poets, who lived and died in Spain, into the contemporary colloquial). In 1982, Amichai was awarded the Israel Prize, the citation for which referred to 'the revolutionary change in poetry's language' that he had helped bring about. Though there is no Israeli laureateship, Amichai was closest to being the nation's poet, in a practical sense as well, as we have seen, in that he was among the foremost creators of the modern Hebrew language. In a 1992 interview, he remarked of himself: 'I am, in a way, like the State of Israel – I have a poem which says, "when I was young, the country was young" . . . My personal history has coincided with a larger history. For me it's always been one and the same.'

Hughes got to know of Amichai's work in 1964, when the first issue of *Modern Poetry in Translation* was being prepared. An English-language poet living in Israel, the late Dennis Silk (see 'Dennis was Very Sick', below) submitted a few versions of Amichai's poetry which subsequently appeared in the first issue of *MPT*. Hughes shortly after began to work on more poems with Assia Gutmann. It was these translations that comprised Amichai's first book in English. As Hughes wrote later: '[Amichai is] the poet whose books I still open most often, most often take on a journey, most often return to when the whole business of writing anything natural, real and satisfying, seems impossible . . . The effect his poetry has on me is to give me my own life – to open it up somehow, to make it all available to me afresh, to uncover all kinds of riches in every moment of it, and to free me from my mental prisons.' There was a particular affinity between the two poets (see Appendix 6 for excerpts from letters between Hughes and Amichai).

About his translations, Ted Hughes, in his Introduction to *Amen*, remarked that what he wanted to do was to 'preserve above all [. . .] the tone and cadence of Amichai's own voice speaking in English, which seems to me marvellously true to the poetry . . .' Amichai supplied Hughes with English versions, which Hughes revised, often quite minimally. They met several times and corresponded, but apparently their consultations were as often verbal, on the phone.

Hughes saw Amichai as the 'chief character in a drama', the drama of his own life, which of course is intimately linked to the life of a new nation, ancient as that new nation may be. As he quite frequently remarked, he was more drawn to Amichai's poetry, even if he had access to it only through translation, than to that of any other contemporary writer. At one point he said that he was even beginning to study Hebrew. Amichai functioned, it seems to me, as a kind of guide for Hughes through the Biblical lands. Amichai tells the story of himself, but the context, a historical one, remains quite impersonal. Hughes was intrigued by this double aspect of the Israeli poet's work.

The poems below are all taken from *Selected Poems* (Faber, 2000), though they first appeared in earlier collections.

A Weeping Mouth

A weeping mouth and a laughing mouth
in terrible battle before a silent crowd.

Each gets hold of the mouth, tears and bites
the mouth, smashes it to shreds and bitter blood.

Till the weeping mouth surrenders and laughs,
till the laughing mouth surrenders and weeps.

[TH and Yehuda Amichai]

My Parents' Migration

And my parents' migration has not yet calmed in me.
My blood goes on shaking at its walls.
As the bowl after it is set down.
And my parents' migration has not yet calmed in me.
Winds continually over stones.
Earth forgets the footsteps of those who walk.
An awful fate. Stumps of talk after midnight.
An achievement, a retreat. Night reminds
And day forgets.
My eyes which have looked a long time into a vast desert,
Are a little calmed. One woman. The rules of a game
Nobody had ever completely explained. The laws of pain
    and weight.

Even now my heart
Makes only a bare living
With its daily love.
My parents in their migration
On the crossroads where I am forever orphaned,
Too young to die, too old to play.
The weariness of the miner
The emptiness of the quarry
In one body.
Archaeology of the future
Museums of what is still to happen.
And my parents' migration has not yet calmed in me,
And from bitter peoples I learned bitter languages
For my silence among the houses
Which are always
Like ships.

Already my veins, my tendons
Are a tangle of ropes I will never undo
Finally, my own
Death
And an end to my parents' migration.

[TH and Assia Gutmann]

Dennis was Very Sick

Dennis was very sick.
His face retreated
But his eyes advanced from it
With great courage
As in a war
When the fresh reinforcements
Pass on their way to the front
The retreating columns of the beaten.

He has to get healthy soon.
He is like our bank,
In which we deposited all we had in our heart.
He is like Switzerland,
Filled with banks.

Already he is smoking one cigarette,
Trembling a little,
And as it should be with a true poet,
He puts the burned matches
Back into the box.

[TH and Yehuda Amichai]

How Did a Flag

How did a flag come into being?
Let's assume that in the beginning
there was something whole, which was
then torn into two pieces, both big enough
for two battling armies.

Or like the ragged striped fabric
of a beach chair in an abandoned
little garden of my childhood,
flapping in the wind. This
too could be a flag making you arise
to follow it or to weep at its side,
to betray it or to forget.

I don't know. In my wars
no flag-bearer marched in front
of the grey soldiers in clouds of dust and smoke.
I've seen things starting as spring,
ending up with hasty retreat
in pale dunes.
I'm far away from all that, like one
who in the middle of a bridge
forgets both its ends
and remains standing there
bent over the railing
to look down into the streaming water:
This too is a flag.

[TH and Yehuda Amichai]

On My Return

I will not be greeted on my return
by children's voices, or by the barking
of a loyal dog, or by blue smoke rising
as it happens in legends.

There won't happen for me any 'and he
lifted his eyes' – as
in the Bible – 'and behold'.

I have crossed the border of being an orphan.
It's a long time since they called me
an ex-serviceman.
I'm not protected anymore.

But I have invented the dry weeping.
And who has invented this
has invented the beginning of the world's end,
the crack and the tumbling down and the end.

[TH and Yehuda Amichai]

Mayor

It's sad
To be the Mayor of Jerusalem.
It is terrible.
How can any man be the mayor of a city like that?

What can he do with her?
He will build, and build, and build.

And at night
The stones of the hills round about
Will crawl down
Towards the stone houses,
Like wolves coming
To howl at the dogs
Who have become men's slaves.

[TH and Assia Gutmann]

I've Filtered out of the Book of Esther

I've filtered out of the Book of Esther the residue
of vulgar joy, and out of the Book of Jeremiah
the howl of pain in the guts. And out of the
Song of Songs the endless search for love,
and out of the Book of Genesis the dreams
and Cain, and out of Ecclesiastes
the despair and out of the Book of Job – Job.
And from what was left over I pasted for myself a new
    Bible.
Now I live censored and pasted and limited and in peace.

A woman asked me last night in the darkened street
about the well-being of another woman
who had died before her time, and not in anyone's
      time.
Out of great tiredness I answered her:
She's fine, she's fine.

[TH and Yehuda Amichai]

Luxury

My uncle is buried at Sheik Baadar.
The other one is scattered in the Carpathian mountains.

My father is buried in the Synhedria,
My grandmother on the Mount of Olives
And all their forefathers
Are buried in the ruined Jewish cemeteries in the villages of
      Lower Franconia,
Near rivers and forests which are not Jerusalem.

My father's father kept heavy-eyed
Jewish cows in their sheds below the kitchen –

And rose at four in the morning.
I inherited his early rising,
My mouth bitter with nightmares:
I attend to my bad dreams.

Grandfather, Grandfather,
Chief Rabbi of my life,
As you sold unleavened bread on the Passover Eve,
Sell my pains –
So they stay in me, even ache, but not mine,
Not my property.

So many tombstones are scattered behind me –
Names, engraved like the names of long-abandoned railway
      stations.
How shall I cover all these distances,
How can I keep them connected?

I can't afford such an intricate network.
It's a luxury.

[TH and Assia Gutmann]

Once a Great Love

Once a great love cut my life in two.
The first part goes on twisting
at some other place like a snake cut in two.

The passing years have calmed me
and brought healing to my heart and rest to my eyes.

And I'm like someone standing in
the Judean desert, looking at a sign:
'Sea Level'.
He cannot see the sea, but he knows.

Thus I remember your face everywhere
at your 'face level'.

[TH and Yehuda Amichai]

One Sees All Kinds of Things

'One sees all kinds of things,' said the Swedish
officer observing at the armistice line.
'All kinds of things,' and said nothing more.

'One sees a lot of things,' said the old
shoeshine man by the Jaffa gate
when a Swedish girl in a very short dress
stood above him, without looking at him
with her proud eyes.

The prophet who looked into the opening heaven saw,
and so did God, 'all kinds of things' down there beyond the
    smoke,
and the surgeon saw when he cut open a cancerous belly
and closed it again.

'One sees all kinds of things,' said
our ancestor Jacob on his bed after the blessing
which took his last strength. 'All kinds
of things,' and he turned
towards the wall and he died.

[TH and Yehuda Amichai]

Ibn Gabirol

Sometimes pus
Sometimes a poem.

Something always bursts out
And always pain.

My father was a tree in a forest of fathers
Covered in green cotton wool.

Oh, widows of the flesh, orphans of the blood,
I must escape.

Eyes sharp as tin-openers
Opened heavy secrets.

But through the wound on my chest
God peers into the world.

I am the door
To his apartment.

[TH and Assia Gutmann]

National Thoughts

You: trapped in the homeland of the Chosen People,
On your head a Cossack's fur hat,
Child of their pogroms.
'After these words.' Always,
Or, for instance, your face: slanting eyes,
Pogrom-Year eyes. Your cheekbones, high,

Hetman's cheekbones, Hetman the rabble-king.
Hassid dancing, dutiful, you, naked on a rock in the early
    evening by the canopies of water at Ein Geddi
With eyes closed and your body open like hair.

After these words, 'Always.'
Every day I know the miracle of
Jesus walking upon the waters,
I walk through my life without drowning.

To speak, now, in this tired language
Torn from its sleep in the Bible –
Blinded, it lurches from mouth to mouth –
The language which described God and the Miracles,
    Says:
Motor car, bomb, God.

The squared letters wanted to stay closed,
Every letter a locked house,
To stay and to sleep in it for ever.

[TH and Assia Gutmann]

Seneca

Lucius Annaeus Seneca (4 BC–AD 65) was a prominent Roman statesman, stoic philosopher and tragic poet, as well as a noted rhetorician. Born in Spain into a wealthy family, he came to Rome in early childhood. He was celebrated as an orator and writer, his career getting under way in the reign of the emperor Caligula. Later he was tutor to the emperor Nero and on the latter's accession became very influential for a while. His life ended, however, in disaster with his being accused of complicity in a plot and ordered to commit suicide. Seneca's speeches have not survived but much of his verse and prose (treatises and letters) has, including his tragedies, which were designed for reading and recitation rather than staged performances. Most of the plays are drawn from Greek mythology, but Seneca uses an elaborate rhetoric, alien to the Greek model, and dwells on gory details. He was also appreciated for his epigrammatic style and fondness for paradox. His drama was familiar in the sixteenth-century when Greek tragedy was scarcely known, and all the plays were translated into English in the Tudor period. T. S. Eliot wrote two important essays on Seneca, 'Seneca in Elizabethan Translation' and 'Shakespeare and the Stoicism of Seneca' (1927).

Of the plays Seneca left behind, at least eight, including *Oedipus*, have survived. All are adapted from the work of other playwrights. *Oedipus* being based on Sophocles' *Oedipus Tyrannus*. Seneca, however, freely discarded scenes, rearranging and using material as he saw fit. His plays profoundly influenced the development of the tragic form in the age of Shakespeare. Seneca was perhaps best known for his scenes of violence and horror, *Oedipus* furnishing several examples of this. His fascination with magic, death and the supernatural was imitated by many Elizabethan playwrights.

Hughes's adaptation of Seneca's *Oedipus* was first performed by the National Theatre Company in March 1968, produced and designed by Peter Brook, with John Gielgud in the title role and Irene Worth as Queen Jocasta. A version had been commissioned from David Turner, but (as Hughes put it in his Introduction): 'Peter Brook had clear ideas about the type of production he wanted, and when he found the translation [by Turner] did not quite suit them he invited me in to go over it and adapt it [. . .] and after some tentative false starts, we found the only way forward was for me to go back to the original Seneca, eking out my Latin with a Victorian crib and so make a completely new translation.' Brook, in fact, got the actors to study the play in this 'Victorian crib', a version by Frank Justus Miller first published in 1917, which Hughes describes as 'being extremely weighty and extremely literal' (from Hughes's unpublished account of his dealings with the National Theatre). As Hughes notes further: 'I was in complete sympathy with Peter Brook's guiding idea, which was to make a text that would release whatever inner power this story, in its plainest, bluntest form, still has, and to unearth, if we could, the ritual possibilities within it.'

Charles Marowitz (see 'Seneca's Oedipus', from *Confessions of a Counterfeit Critic*, London, 1977, in *Classical Tragedy Greek and Roman: Eight Plays*, edited by Robert W. Corrigan, New York, 1990, a collection which contains David Anthony Turner's version of the play) characterises Brook's production as an 'oratorio . . . , for what Brook has done is to treat the Senecan text like a richly-textured piece of music with syncopation, parallel harmonies and counterpoints. The sound components of the words have been carefully organised to create a maximum degree of tonal variety. Actors hiss, throb, vibrate and intone throughout the evening. Individual speeches are constantly invaded by group sounds, frequently mickey-mousing narrative descriptions, occasionally providing a subtle counterpoint to speech.' This unorthodox approach evidently appealed to Hughes – his use of spaces to indicate pauses suggests that the text is to be read almost like a musical score – as an experiment in ritual theatre, for which he, as writer of the text or librettist, had to create a new kind of English. While Marowitz is critical of Brook's treatment of Seneca ('. . . Brook has devised an ingenious theatrical overlay, the principles of which belong to his own aesthetic rather than the need or purposes of his text'), Hughes seems to have been largely sympathetic to Brook's ideas.

In an interview (March 1982) transcribed by Ann Skea (see www.zeta.org. au/~annskea/ABC1.htm), Hughes, referring to Peter Brook's interest in Seneca's *Oedipus*, emphasises that it was Brook's vision, not his own. He refers to 'a very primitive raw shape of a drama' as being what interested Brook, adding, however, that 'it was my idea in the translation to do that – to find some way of discarding the ornateness and the stateliness . . . and to bring out some quite thin but raw presentation of the real core of the play. And in doing that, I shed every mythological reference, which shortened the play by about a third. I shortened every sentence. In fact, I discarded sentence structure . . . I didn't have to imagine a whole new dramatic language . . . the actors were performing my translation all the time I was translating. So I came up first of all with one version of a part of it, that seemed to me very bare, and to have got through to something essential, and they began to perform and rehearse it, and I began to feel . . . [we] were driving towards some intense situation in the middle of the play – that this language began to seem too elaborate. And I stripped it again . . . and this process went on and on and on. I went through many, many drafts until, finally, I was down to about 250 words – that's what it felt like – and a rigid, sort of ugly language, which somehow seemed to come out of this central situation . . . And [we] ended up, finally, with a very short play which just was about . . . this central situation, this little naked knot. . . . So the play finally just had to be performed like an express train.' He did, however, have doubts, and even wondered whether it might not have been preferable to approach it in quite the opposite way, elaborating still further on the language, 'so the whole thing would have been much more statuesque . . .'

As Hughes writes in his Introduction to the published edition of *Oedipus* (Faber, 1969): 'The figures in Seneca's *Oedipus* are Greek only by convention; by nature they are more primitive than aboriginals. They are a spider people, scuttling among hot stones.' Seneca produces 'a series of epic descriptions that contain the raw dream of Oedipus, the basic, poetic, mythical substance of the fable . . .' He concludes: 'In Seneca's hands, in other words, this story becomes something close to the scenario of a mystery play, in the religious sense.'

The plot preceding the action of the play is as follows: An oracle has foretold that King Laius of Thebes will perish by his own son's hands. Accordingly, when a son is born he pierces his foot with a nail (hence the name Oedipus, meaning swell-foot) and has him exposed on a mountainside, presuming that he will perish. The shepherd given this task, however entrusts the boy to a wandering herdsman of Polybus, King of Corinth, and Oedipus is brought up as the latter's son. Later he flees Corinth to escape the destiny allotted to him, thinking that he is destined to kill his supposed father, Polybus. En route he, in fact, does kill an old man, who turns out to be Laius, and on arriving in Theban territory guesses the riddle of the Sphinx, thus destroying the monster which has been harassing Thebes. The grateful Thebans make him husband of Jocasta, widowed queen of the recently slain Laius. Subsequently, a pestilence afflicts Thebes. Oedipus has sent Creon, Jocasta's brother, to consult the oracle, which is where the play begins. Oedipus curses the killer of Laius (this being himself!). When Jocasta learns who her husband really is, she hangs herself and Oedipus blinds himself. After wandering for many years, guided by his daughter Antigone, Oedipus comes to Colonus in Attica, where the Erinyes hound him to death.

Note that Hughes uses spaces between words to indicate pauses, rather than using conventional punctuation. See Appendix 7 for versions of a passage by Miller, Turner and Alexander Nevyle, the adolescent Tudor translator of Seneca's plays.

Excerpt 1
(Act One. In his opening speech, Oedipus describes the fear that drives him.)

> [. . .] but the fear
> came with me   my shadow   into his kingdom to
> this throne   and it grew   till now it surrounds
> me   fear   I stand in it   like a blind man in
> darkness even now   what is fate preparing for me   surely I
> see that   how could I be mistaken this plague
> slaughtering everything that lives no matter what
> men trees flies no matter it spares me   why
> what final disaster is it saving me for
> the whole nation guttering   the last dregs of its life
> no order left   ugly horrible deaths in every doorway
> every path wherever you look funeral after funeral
> endless terror and sobbing and in the middle of it all
> I stand here   untouched   the man marked down by
> the god   for the worst fate of all   a man hated
> and accused by the god   still unsentenced

Excerpt 2
(Act One. Jocasta, urging Oedipus to be a true king, to take heart, shows herself as able to accept the odds, the birth of a son, whatever the prognostications.)

> When I carried my sons
> I carried them for death   I carried them for the throne
> [. . .]
> I knew the thing in my womb was going to have to pay for
>   the whole past
> I knew the future was waiting for him like a greedy god a
>   maneater in a cave
> was going to ask for everything   happiness strength and
>   finally life
> As if no other man existed   I carried him for this for pain and
>   for fear

for hard sharp metal   for the cruelty of other men and his
    own cruelty
I carried him for disease
for rottenness and dropping to pieces
I carried him for death bones dust   I knew
but I carried him not only for this I carried him to be king
    of this
and my blood didn't pause
didn't hesitate in my womb
considering the futility
it didn't falter reckoning the odds   it poured on
into him   blood from my toes my finger ends
blind blood   blood from my gums and eyelids
blood from the roots of my hair
blood from before any time began
it flowed into the knot of his bowels, into the knot of his
    muscles
the knot of his brain
my womb tied everything together every corner of the earth
    and the heavens
and every trickle of the dead past
twisted it all into shape inside me
what was he   what wasn't he
the question was unasked
and what was I   what cauldron was I
what doorway was I   what cavemouth
what spread my legs and lifted my knees
was he squeezing to hide
was I running to escape
the strength of the whole earth
pushed him through my body and out
it split me open and I saw the blood jump out after him
was I myself   but what was he
a bag of blood   a bag of death
a screaming mouth
was it asking a question
he was a king's son   he was a man's shape
he was perfect

Excerpt 3

(*Act Two. King Oedipus, in dialogue with Creon, Jocasta's brother, calls for expiation for the murder of his predecessor Laius, so as to bring about deliverance from the scourge that is afflicting Thebes and for which, of course, he himself is unwittingly responsible.*)

> the movers the guides the lawgivers   are above
> they are demanding expiation for this murder
> vengeance for Laius   the King of Thebes
> where is the man
>
> you great gods   you who choose Kings from among
> men and set them up and keep them in power
> come down and hear these words   you who made
> this whole Universe and the laws we have to live and
> die in   hear me   and you   great burning
> watchers   who look after the seasons of this earth
> who give sap and blood its strength   who pace out
> the centuries   and you who govern darkness   and
> you   muscle of the earth   who move and speak
> in the winds and in water   and you who manage the
> dead   be with me now   hear these words I
> speak now [. . .]

Excerpt 4

(*Act Three. Creon reports how Laius, who had been called up from the dead so he could tell who had killed him, spoke the following words.*)

> you insane family of Cadmus
> you will never stop slaughtering each other
> finish it now   rip your children with your own hands put
>   an end to your blood now
> because worse is coming
> an evil too detestable to name is squatting on the throne of
>   Thebes
> my country rots   but it isn't the gods
> it is this   a son and a mother

knotted and twisted together   a son and a mother
blood flowing back together in the one sewer
it isn't the wind   fevers from the south of your dried out
    earth   the drought and its scorching dust
those things are innocent
it is your king
blinded in the wrong that got him his throne   blinded
to his own origins   blind to the fixed gods   the
loathed son of that same queen who now swells under
    him   the Queen   yes   worse than him   the
Queen   and her womb that chamber of hell
which began it all   he pushed his way back there
where he began   worse than an animal   he buried
his head in there   there where he first came
screaming out   and brought new brothers for himself
out of his own mother's body   horrible tentacles
of evil   a bloodier tangle than his own sphinx

you   clutching that sceptre which does not belong
to you   I am the man you murdered for it   your
father   still not avenged   but I'll bring a brides-
maid to your marriage   a fury to bind you and
your mother together with a whiplash   I shall
disembowel your city I shall start your sons
butchering each other   I shall rip your whole infernal
lineage out by the roots   men of Thebes   get rid
of this monster   drive him away   no matter where
only let him go quickly   let him take that deadly
shadow of his elsewhere   then your streams will
recover   and the roots will revive and blossom come
again and the fruit swell   a pure air will sweep
through the land   and the grief the pestilence the
deathpains the horror the death   they will all follow
his footsteps [. . .]

Excerpt 5
(*Act Four. Oedipus acknowledges that he is the cause of the pestilence. Through remorseless interrogations, despite Jocasta's protests, he has dragged out the truth.*)

> [. . .] I am the cancer
> at the roots of this city   and in your blood and in
> the air   I should have died in the womb
> suffocated   inside there   drowned in my
> mother's blood   come out dead   that first day
> before anything [. . .]

Excerpt 6
(*Act Four. Chorus tells the story of Icarus and Daedalus, like Oedipus powerless to avoid their destiny.*)

> If only our fate were ours to choose   you would see me on
> quiet waters   where the airs are gentle   a full sail but a
> light wind   no more than a breath   easy voyage   that is
> best   no blast no smashed rigging no flogging downwind into
> cliffs   under surge nothing recovered   no vanishing in
> mid ocean
>
> give me a quiet voyage   neither under cliffs nor too far out
> on the black water where the depths ocean   the middle
>   course
> is the safe one   the only life   easily on   to a calm end
> surrounded by gains
>
> foolish Icarus   he thought he could fly
> it was a dream
> tried to crawl across the stars
> loaded with his crazy dream   his crazy paraphernalia
> the wings the wax and the feathers
> up and up and up
> saw eagles beneath him   saw his enormous shadow on the
>   clouds beneath him
> met the sun face to face
> fell

his father Daedalus was wiser   he flew lower
he kept under clouds   in the shadow of the clouds
the same crazy equipment   but the dream different
till Icarus dropped past him   out of the belly of a cloud
past him
down
through emptiness
a cry   dwindling
a splash

tiny in the middle of the vast sea

Excerpt 7
(*Act Five. A slave recounts how Oedipus blinded himself.*)

suddenly he began to weep   everything that had been
torment suddenly it was sobbing   it shook his whole
body and he shouted   is weeping all I can give
can't my eyes give any more   let them go with their
tears   let them go   eyeballs too   everything
out   is this enough for you you frozen gods of
marriage   is it sufficient   are my eyes enough

Excerpt 8
(*Act Five. Chorus draws the moral: fate cannot be avoided.*)

Fate is the master of everything   it is vain to fight against
    fate
from the beginning to the end the road is laid
    down   human
scheming is futile   worries are futile   prayers are futile
sometimes a man wins   sometimes he loses
who decides whether he loses or wins
it has all been decided long ago elsewhere
it is destiny
not a single man can alter it
all he can do is let it happen

the good luck the bad luck everything that happens
everything that seems to toss our days up and down
it is all there from the first moment
it is all there   tangled in the knotted mesh of causes
helpless to change itself
even the great god lies there entangled
helpless in the mesh of causes
and the last day lies there tangled with the first
a man's life is a pattern on the floor   like a maze
it is all fixed   he wanders in the pattern
no prayer can alter it
or help him to escape it   nothing

then fear can be the end of him
a man's fear of his fate is often his fate
leaping to avoid it   he meets it

Excerpt 9

(*Act Five. Oedipus declares that he will leave Thebes. In a beatific
vision of prosperity he predicts that now all will be well.*)

[. . .] I am taking my curse off you
now you can hope again   lift your faces   now you
will see the skies alter   and the sun and the grass
everything will change now   all you stretched out
hoping only for death your face pressed to your graves
look up   if you can move now   if you can breathe
suck in this new air   it will cure all the sickness
go and bury your dead now without fear   because
the contagion is leaving your land I am taking it with
me   I am taking it away   fate   remorseless
my enemy   you are the friend I choose   come with
me
pestilence   ulcerous agony   blasting consumption
plague terror   plague blackness despair
welcome   come with me   you are my guides
lead me

Orghast

Seneca's Oedipus inaugurated Hughes's collaboration with Peter Brook, which culminated in *Orghast*, the first major public project of Brook's Paris-based International Centre for Theatre Research. *Orghast* was scripted for a 1971 performance at the Fifth Annual Festival of the Arts, the Shiraz Festival, in Persepolis, where it was performed at the ruined palace of Darius the Great, after having been evolved by the company in rehearsal in Paris and then in Iran.

The play draws on *Prometheus Bound* (the first part of a lost trilogy by Aeschylus), but is written in a language invented by Hughes for the purpose, although incorporating passages of *Avesta* (an ancient Persian language, the language of the Zoroastrian Holy Scriptures) and of Classical Greek. It is based on the myth of Prometheus, the Titan, who stole fire from heaven and gave it to humankind and suffered the wrath of Zeus, being chained to a rock for eternity, his liver eaten daily by a vulture and regenerating itself. As retold by Hughes, the story is enacted within the body of the Titan, as he is chained to his rock in agony.

'The Conference of the Birds', a Persian Sufi story (see Farud ud-Din Attar, *The Conference of the Birds*, translated with an introduction by Afkham Darbandi and Dick Davis, Penguin, 1984), was a sort of repertory piece for Brook's international group of actors in Paris. It could be performed impromptu, as an exercise or to entertain visitors, with no words to remember, only a scenario and sounds. Whether it was already in the repertory before Hughes's involvement is uncertain, but in any case he came up with his own sounds for it and it seems likely that these sounds were, so to speak, ur-*Orghast*.

Hughes's interest in translation dates from at least the late 1950s, and he was fascinated by the search for an *ursprache* (to use Walter Benjamin's term in his landmark essay 'The Task of the Translator', a translation of which appeared in *Delos* (2, 1968; Austin, Texas), a journal with which Hughes was familiar). Hughes's programme note to the first Poetry International reading, in London in 1967, suggests these preoccupations (see also Appendix 1): 'However rootedly-national in detail it may be, poetry is less and less the prisoner of its own language . . . Or perhaps it is only now being heard for what, among other things, it is – a Universal language of understanding, coherent behind the many languages, in which we can all hope to meet.' He returned to the theme much later, when, as Poet Laureate, he addressed the Second Asian Poetry Festival in Bangladesh. Here he talked of the need to 'find in poetry a single common language of fellow feeling . . . of shared essential humanity' (from Hughes's manuscript notes for this speech). For Hughes, translation, rather than being a weapon of colonialism as post-colonial critics have often depicted it, was potentially a means of rapprochement, of cross-cultural understanding.

It is at least arguably this belief that underlies his interest in the language experiment represented by *Orghast*. He was particularly drawn to the theatre, especially to radical work by such as Antonin Artaud, who envisaged 'total immediacy', 'a wholly auditory language'; similarly, Grotowski's views on acting, as interpreted by Brook, appealed to him: the determination to short-circuit conventional responses, to sidestep reliance on technological wizardry and return to the expressive potential of the human voice and body.

Hughes found himself broadly in tune with what Peter Brook was attempting, and their collaboration in the *Oedipus* and then in *Orghast* were key moments in his own development. In conversation with Clive Wilmer (Clive Wilmer, *Poets Talking: Poet of the Month Interviews from BBC Radio 3*, 1994), he suggests what he felt was to be learnt from these experiments: 'I think it sharpened my sense of the mosaic quality of verse . . . When language begins to operate like that [i.e., the work with Brook] one's attention or the meaning is somehow pitched beyond the superficial syntactical meaning.' In his Seneca translation, Hughes had worked towards a reduced language, in which gesture was nakedly apparent. As Sandie Byrne comments (*The Poetry of Ted Hughes: A Reader's Guide to Essential Criticism*, 2000): '[T]he work he carried out on Seneca's *Oedipus* seems to have been a kind of first attempt . . . In fact, Ted Hughes rewrote the text in "spare, asyntactic and not always comprehensible" language. It was nevertheless recognisable English, punctuation being replaced by large gaps, creating a multitude of semantic ambiguities and foregrounding the sounds of the words – a style which calls to mind Joyce's "stream of consciousness".' Paul Bentley (*The Poetry of Ted Hughes: Language, Illusion and Beyond*, 1998), notes: '[W]hat Hughes was aiming for here was a purely "semiotic" language, a language of "vocal or kinetic rhythm", stripped of its figurative or conceptual function.'

In an interview, Hughes commented on his readiness to abandon literary English: 'English was hopeless. It could never have come near it . . . The first vocabulary of *Orghast* was a language purged of the haphazard associations of English, which continually tries to supplant experience and truth with the mechanisms of its own autonomous life.' The connection here with the 'super-ugly' style of *Crow* is not accidental. In an interview with Tom Stoppard (Tom Stoppard, 'Orghast', *TLS*, 1 October 1971), Hughes remarks: 'I was interested in the possibilities of a language of tones and sounds, without specific conceptual or perceptual meanings . . .' In the same interview, he notes that 'the best words are words you invent immediately, your mind fixed on the thing or state you want to express.' He wonders at this, but clearly takes it as indicating that he was on the track of something authentic.

Also in the Stoppard interview, Hughes gives his own version of the Persian experiment as a whole. 'When I went to Persia with Peter Brook [. . .] there was no basic play – nothing – it was left up to us, and he just asked me to make a play out of *Prometheus Bound* [Aeschylus], *Life is a Dream* [Calderón], and then all sorts of other little stories that he gradually put onto it, and the texts of the *Avesta* – the early Persian religious texts. So on that material we began to devise a performance – a sort of show.' From this it is evident not only that *Orghast* drew on diverse sources, but also that it was very much a collaborative project. He continues, noting the similarity with operatic productions: 'We had to invent a long series of small scenes. And Peter Brook's basic idea was to make it up of many little bits and pieces of the original language or languages. He found a professor who had reconstructed the pronunciation of Ancient Greek; he had chunks of Spanish; he had a Persian lady who'd reconstructed the original pronunciation of the *Avesta* . . . The sense had to come from the situations that we devised out of these basics. And eventually we did devise a kind of play . . . But the original languages were too stiff to use, really, and also I could work more easily, if I devised my scenes. I simply wrote them in another language – so I invented a language.' A bit later, distinguishing also between drama and poetry, he comments: 'I was interested in the possibilities of a language of tones and sounds, without specific conceptual or perceptual meanings, long before, but for drama not for poetry. In poetry this sort of experiment remains meaningless, for such a language needs a body of precise but unexpressed meaning behind it – such as is supplied by religious intention (as in mantras, etc.) or by action.'

In a revealing interview with Stan Correy and Robyn Ravlich in March 1982 (first broadcast in 1982 by Radio National and ABC, Australia, and transcribed by Ann Skea – see www.zeta.org.au/~annskea/ABC1.htm), Hughes remarks on his adaptation of Seneca's *Oedipus*, with its pared down English, and *Orghast*, where he developed an 'almost unconscious language of utterance': 'I think . . . everybody felt . . . an enormously elaborate literary tradition had completely swamped any natural expression, any possibility of stating all kinds of attitudes and feelings that had developed under the surface and were obviously wanting to emerge.' One is reminded of his interest in the 'minimal' language of Eastern European poetry, in János Pilinszky's 'poor language', in Yehuda Amichai's English versions of his Hebrew originals. 'We're still in a movement . . . where there are writers who are trying to simplify language and draw it as plainly as possible back to spoken language – back to an oral tradition; and parallel with it there are several schools of language that are elaborating it and making it almost a freakish art-object . . . And so we've a continual chronic state of trying to renew a language, that we're continually somehow overburdening with literary effects and devices . . .' In response to a question about the renewal of language as he saw it, Hughes defines what he saw as the task of the translator and how he arrived at the elemental language of his translation of Seneca's rhetoric. This leads directly into his further and far more radical language experiment with *Orghast*.

But how did Hughes actually set about the task of creating a language? He describes the process rather disarmingly. 'What made it easier . . . was that the play itself provided a closed system of themes. The basic idea being Prometheus and the vulture, and the basic myth of the early Persian religion, and the *Life is a Dream* – the cast-out prince in the prison who is put back on the throne for a day or two . . . I tied all these together in one big system and that gave you certain basic ideas and basic images, which I used as the main ideas for my language. So the main idea in the whole play . . . was just fire. So fire was my first word. And I invented a word for fire. And then another big image was the sun; my word for sun was made out of my word for fire and a word for eating, and so on . . . I could then develop a whole language by a sort of metaphorical process – of making bundles of the sounds that composed these other ideas, so that any particular word that I needed in my text, I could fit together out of the sounds that I already had.' He commented in the Wilmer interview: '[T]o begin with we had no language at all. We were just using bird-cries (based on Attar's *The Conference of the Birds*). We were hoping to force the actors back into resources behind verbal expressiveness, back into some sort of musical or other kind of expressiveness. And in the course of this I wrote one scene about the vulture visiting Prometheus on his crag. I wanted to write a text of some kind so that I could organise the music of it. So I just invented about half-a-dozen words and automatically . . . I made each syllable represent what I considered to be one of the central ideas of the drama.'

However, he noticed that this process became too rigid, as the actors began to use it just as another langauge, 'so I began to recompose the language and improvise it. In the end I abandoned the language altogether and I wrote just in sounds, which I composed through the particular scene. We composed it musically.' (Here he returns to his earlier Artaudian notion of the operatic nature of their work; one is also reminded of his early interest in operatic composition, in relation to his work on the *Bardo* oratorio.) The participation of the actors in the creation of the play is then described: '[W]e orchestrated the sound. And we could only do that when we had the actual scene developing in front of us. The actors knew the way through the scene; they knew approximately the drift of feeling and meaning behind the sounds, and from that point we could begin to cut down the sounds, so that we ended up with a play of cries and whispers and chatterings – really a sort of vocal musical piece that went with a very active and, in the end, a very effective action.'

Sometimes Hughes chanced, as it were, on a word which had real antecedents: 'My word for "light" – *hoan* – was a completely blind invention but it turns out to mean a ray of light in Farsi. My "woman of light" I called Ussa, which was just a provisional name until we discovered it meant "dawn" in Sanskrit and is close to the old Farsi word for "fire", now only used as a girl's name. There were quite a few of that sort of coincidence . . . The good words are the words you invent immediately – blind – your mind completely fixed on the thing or state you want to express. Out of these root words, you compound others. Some of these are good, others not so good. Afterwards, the words I invented blind turned out to be compounds of the first roots I established.'

The word *Orghast* itself is the product of two roots, *org* and *ghast*. It is the name for 'the fire of being', and metaphorically for 'sun'. Anthony Smith explains the origin of the word *Orghast* as derived from certain root sounds to which Hughes had given specific meanings (see Ossia Trilling, 'Playing with Words at Persepolis', *Theatre Quarterly*, Vol. 11, No. 5, London, Jan–March, 1972). Thus *Orghast* is made up of the words *orga* (being), *ghast* (flame), and *asta* (ice).

Summing up, Anthony Smith calls *Orghast* a language that is rather 'Gaelic in feeling', that tries to express itself physiologically. 'Several of the syllables were tried out on the tongue both by Hughes and by the actors, to see what effect they might have on the speaker, as well as on the listener. Several words eventually acquired their final shape and form and, what is more important, their mode of utterance, in the course of constant trial and error on the part of the actors, hence the analogy to musical sound . . . Other roots were, *gr* (eat), *ull* (swallow) and *kr* (devour), and it is not difficult to share in the sense of equivalence between the change of root and the change of "mental state" in three different kinds of eating. *Urg* was death, *uss* light, *bruss* strength, and *gra* fire.'

Hughes himself observes that, contrary to appearance, *Orghast* was in a way closer to ordinary speech than most literary speech. '[S]o *Orghast* was really one step beyond *Oedipus* in stripping off the intrusive, formal, merely communicative or intercommunicative element of language – that intellectual and loaded side of language – to a system of noises – music – that people make to each other.' ('An ordinary person's speech is infinitely more alive and musical just as sounds and as the note of a voice that you interpret very, very accurately . . .')

The relevance of all this to translation may not be immediately apparent, except that Hughes addresses this issue specifically: 'In literature you hear it all, but translated, as though literature were a more formal ordering and translation of what you hear otherwise. But in literature, you don't hear it just as language, you hear it as a system of attitudes and feelings and ideas and so on. Whereas in ordinary speech you hear it as a purely musical, animal chord which you respond to immediately – but you understand in a very complicated way . . .' It is almost as if he were translating back *from* translations to what underlies them.

If *Orghast*, in its esotericism, can hardly be claimed to have solved the problem of preserving the colloquial expressiveness of ordinary speech, it is at least suggestive of a line of approach. No excerpt can give more than the slenderest notion of a text that was part of a total spectacle, as performed in the particular circumstances of the Shiraz Festival, for a detailed account of which the reader is directed to A. C. H. Smith's illuminating account, *Orghast at Persepolis* (Eyre Methuen, 1972).

Avesta

(Avesta, *as Smith points out, cannot really be transcribed, but a simulacrum is provided in his book, as follows, 'an invocation to the fecund earth and pregnant women, annotated as Irene Worth [who was also in* Oedipus] *pronounced it. It moves very slowly'.*)

IMAM IMAM IMAM Immaawwmmm – full cheeks, letting the sound go up the nose and around the forehead, as though in a cave
AAT ZAM aaa-at zaawmmm
GENABIS HATHRA YAZAMAIDE gennaawbish
YA NAW BARDAITI YAWSCHA naaooow: yaaaowst*cha*, the last syllable snapped upward in tone, above the tonic note of incantation, and glottally stopped
TOI GENAW AHURA MAZDAW taawi; a-hhura
ASHAT HACHA VAIRYAW TAW vaireeow; taaooow
YAZAMAIDE

Opening section of Part I
(*This is from Ted Hughes's typescript, dated August 1971.*)

Scene: the tomb of Artaxerxes II or III, above the ruins of Persepolis. The cast is scattered, on the platform below, and on the hillside. The audience sits on cushions on both sides of the platform: to one side of the audience, the carved face and entrance of the tomb; on the other side, the view out over Persepolis and the valley, south and west.

LIGHT: (*from above*) continuous call HOAN
MAN: (*from below platform*) GA-VE
LIGHT: call HOAN
MAN: GA-VE
LIGHT: call (*continues under* MOA)
MOA: (*from tomb*) GAVE
CHORUS: AMEM
MAN: GAVE
CHORUS: NEMEM
MOA: GAVE
CHORUS: UKHDHEM
MAN: GAVE
CHORUS: THERETHREM
MOA: GAVE
CHORUS: KHARETFFHEM
MAN: GAVE
CHORUS: KHARETHEM
MAN: GAVE
CHORUS: VASTREM
MOA: GAVE
CHORUS: VEREZYATAM
PROMETHEUS: NE KHARETHAI
CHORUS: TSHUYO
PROMETHEUS: GA-VE
MAN: (*climbing towards platform*) KHSHMAIBYA. GEUS. URVA.
GEREZHDA. KAHMAI. MA. THWAROZHDUM. KE. MA.

HAZASCHA. REMO. AHUSHYA. DERESCHA. TEVISCHA. NOIT.
MOI.

LIGHT: (*part*) VAYO. AURVA. YAZAMAIDE.
VAYO. TAKHMAA. YAZAMAIDE.
VAEM. ZARANYO-VASTREM.

(*The ball of fire starts to descend over front of tomb.*)

[75]

Georges Schehadé

Georges Schehadé (1905–89), poet and playwright, of Lebanese origin, is regarded, along with Ionesco, Adamov and Beckett, as one of the originators of the 'New Theatre' of the 1950s. He began as a poet and was recommended by Eluard to his Surrealist colleagues. Schehadé has himself referred to the 'New Theatre' as a 'Theatre of Poetry'. His play *Histoire de Vasco* (1957) was included in a Penguin volume entitled *Theatre of War* (1956), in a translation by Robert Baldick. With its dreamlike, fairytale atmosphere, it is described as a fantasy comedy, with 'one foot in a Ruritanian setting at the start of the century and one foot in the military realities of today', those realities having to do with the Algerian war. Vasco, the eponymous hero, is a Chaplinesque figure, a timorous yet at the same time courageous *homme moyen universel*. The drama unfolds in a series of tableaux, which lend themselves to poetic treatment.

Hughes's involvement in this project recalls perhaps his involvement much earlier in the never-realised project for an opera based on *The Tibetan Book of the Dead*, the *Bardo Thödol*. With music by Gordon Crosse, *Vasco*, a full-length opera in three acts for seventeen solo voices, chorus and orchestra, was commissioned by the Sadler's Wells Opera Company, and premièred at the London Coliseum in 1974; it was also broadcast on BBC Radio 3 on 21 March 1974.

Excerpt 1
(Act One, Scene 1. Lieutenant September, looking for the barber Vasco, who is to be co-opted in a secret military mission, finds Caesar, father of Vasco's fiancée Marguerite, in a forest, but is encircled by crows, which 'sing mock plainchant in a very nasal voice'.)

    CROWS
        I–E, I–E–O, I–E, A–E–U—I . . .
        NI–E, NIA, NI—E–KA! . . .

Sudden light on various groups of crows. September in shadows.

SEPTEMBER
  Black birds! Those black birds!
  Everywhere I go, the crows are watching.
  This must be crow forest.
  And tonight is like autumn,
  when the world tries to scour itself
  clean with its rainy gales.
  Owls crying, crows staring, roots
  creaking, the forest roaring,
  clouds glooming,
  the world huddled.

CROWS
  NI–E, NI–E–KA! . . .

SEPTEMBER
  Black birds! You black birds!
  Everywhere I go, the crows are watching.
  You crows! You hags!
  Wrap your rags up! Spread your wings!
  Pick up your horrible feet and get out of it!
  Fly, crows, fly!
  (*He draws his pistol and fires. They don't move.*)
  They're all asleep in this infernal wind.

A light goes on in the cart. Caesar appears, dressed in night clothes.

CAESAR
  What? What? What? Who is it?

Excerpt 2
(*Act One, Scene 2. In Vasco's village, Sosso. Dialogue between two old men, Rondo and Troppo, who are busy at a well. Vasco's barbershop can be seen.*)

RONDO
  That's my fifteenth bucketful.
  What do you say to a rest, Troppo?

TROPPO
I say to blazes with the garden, Rondo.

RONDO
Is it worth watering the flowers?

TROPPO
Is it worth watering the garden?

RONDO
My carrots? My radishes? My apples?
My pears? Plums?

TROPPO
My onions? My parsnips? My apricots?
Plums?

BOTH
Ah! What you plant you must look after.
That is one of the laws of God.

TROPPO
Does God plant our sons, or do we?

RONDO
Who plants our sons?

TROPPO
Who planted them?

RONDO
Two toots on a cornet, a bang on a drum!

BOTH
And our village is empty.

RONDO
Not an able body left.

TROPPO
Nothing but crows and widows!

BOTH
War is war: Monsieur Corfan says so.
War is a hoe and our boys are the weeds.
Only the skulking barber blooms!

(They look at Vasco's shop and jeer.)
The darling barber!
The flower barber! . . .

Vasco is seen. He pretends to welcome a customer, flourishes a towel, tests scissors, sets out his things.

Look! He's gone mad!

TROPPO
Pretending to be busy!

RONDO
Barbering the ghosts.

TROPPO
Shaving shadows.

Vasco gives a virtuoso performance. Frequent bows to customers!

Excerpt 3
(Act One, Scene 3. The headquarters of the Mirador, commander-in-chief of the army. The Mirador is conversing with his officers and an aide-de-camp. Vasco is about to leave on a mission.)

SEPTEMBER
He left this morning.

MIRADOR
He's a pleasant little chap . . . this . . . Coco.

SEPTEMBER
Vasco. Coco was a mule.

MIRADOR
Ah yes. Died long ago.

SEPTEMBER
Vasco will soon be dead too!

MIRADOR
Relax! What's one dead man in a war?
How was he instructed?
Was our little barber afraid?

SEPTEMBER

He is taking greetings to Monsieur Bertrand.
Who is trout-fishing in the country.

MIRADOR

Ha! Perhaps that numbskull,
General Bertrand, really *is* trout-fishing!
Did they give him the two-tone whistle?

SEPTEMBER

Yes, but a two-tone whistle won't save him.
He is taking greetings to Monsieur Bertrand;
That's all he knows. He doesn't know that he is
Stepping into a gulf that has already
Swallowed an army!

MIRADOR

It *will* work. It *must* work.

SEPTEMBER

Even while we talk, Vasco goes on walking
Into the reddest of the fire.

MIRADOR

Stop! Stop! Stop! Lieutenant,
You still have lessons to learn.
What *is* a hero?
A hero is a soldier who succeeds . . . is he not?
But the shouting fiery fury,
The fearless ferocious frightener,
He commits the fatal error – for he falls.
He attracts a little bullet – and he falls.
And lies forever dead among the other fools.
A hero is a soldier who succeeds . . . is he not?
The fearful creeping creature,
The butterfly, the frightened snail,
He's the one – every General will agree.
He gets through where all others drop and cry.
And carries out his orders while the
Others feed the crow.

Excerpt 4

(*Act Three, Scene 2. Vasco is sitting on a stool centre stage. It is the enemy outpost. Sergeant Casquot and Lieutenant Barberis are with him. Crows on stage throughout. Later, Marguerite and Caesar appear on the stage.*)

BARBERIS
So you're fond of foliage?
You love the country?
The shade of the trees,
and the song of the birds,
led you through our lines?

VASCO
Yes, mister officer, but I don't know,
if I followed them, or they followed me.

BARBERIS
You were wandering through
this war-torn desolation,
this battle-infested plain, to look for shade?
You were so entranced by the beauties of nature
you never saw a thing?
Not the snout of a rifle?
Not the silver whiskers of a sword?

VASCO
I didn't see the war.

BARBERIS
But the war saw you!

[. . .]

CAESAR
War! War is a matter of crows!
Just hear the theory of it.
Crows must come so wars must come,
The gun is the father, the soldier is the mother.
A soldier falls – there is another crow
sitting on his face. War is the crow's
reproductive system.

MARGUERITE

He was like the dew
on the tip of a blade of grass.
He was thistledown
wandering on a breath
in the midst of a thorn-bush.
A sparrow pecking crumbs off a drum.
He is my heart for ever.
Where is he? Where is he?
He was fifty thousand times
sweeter than my dream.

CAESAR

War is a matter of crows!
Inside every soldier is a crow
waiting to break out and eat him.
War is a matter of crows . . .

János Pilinszky

János Pilinszky (1921–81) was born in Budapest. Besides poetry he published plays, scripts and prose. During World War II, he spent several months in prisoner-of-war camps. From 1946 to 1948 he co-edited *Újhold*, a modernist literary and critical journal. Pilinszky's first collection of poems, *Trapéz és korlát* (Trapeze and Parallel Bars, 1946) won him the prestigious Baumgarten Prize. But with the Communist takeover of Hungary, *Újhold* was banned, and Pilinszky was silenced for over ten years. Subsequently other volumes appeared, and in 1971 he was awarded the Attila József Prize for *Nagyvarosti ikonok* (Metropolitan Icons, 1970). His 1964 oratorio *Sötét mennyország* (Dark Heaven) was set to music by Endre Szervánszky. Pilinszky wrote several avant-garde film scripts somewhat reminiscent of Beckett. In 1977, he published *Conversations with Sheryl Sutton*, a fictional documentation of his relationship with the black American actress (see translation by Peter Jay and Eva Major, 1992).

In her commemorative essay 'Janos Pilinszky: a very different poet' (*New Hungarian Quarterly*, Vol. XXII, No. 84, Budapest, 1981), Ágnes Nemes Nagy, the poet and contemporary of Pilinszky, describes the poems appearing in Pilinszky's first volume as already among the 'future basic poems of the new Hungarian literature'. Pilinszky himself wrote: '[T]he war has ended and the gates of the concentration camps are shut, but I believe that it is precisely this final hush which signifies the supreme reality in our midst today.' Hughes, who met Pilinszky in London at the 1969 Poetry International, wrote of the latter's poetry: 'The silence of artistic integrity "after Auschwitz" is a real thing. The mass of the human evidence of the camps, and of similar situations since, has screwed up the price of "truth" and "reality" and "understanding" beyond what common words seem able to pay. [. . .] The poems are nothing if not part of an appeal to God, but it is a God who seems not to exist. [. . .] A god of absences and negative attributes, quite comfortless. A god in whose Creation the camps and modern physics are equally at home. But this God has the one Almightiness that matters: he is the Truth.'

Hughes was drawn to Pilinszky's poetry partly on account of its confrontation with the destructive facts of human nature, made shockingly apparent during World War II. His access to it was via the English versions made by his friend János Csokits. The bleakness, and at the same time the radiance – radiance and menace in equal proportions, Blakeian or, more precisely, Van Goghian – of Pilinszky's vision moved Hughes. Unlike with Amichai, he was not able to work directly with Pilinszky himself, since the latter's English was too rudimentary, although they could communicate to some extent in French. However, the two poets were in tune with one another; Pilinszky expressed a desire to translate *Crow* into Hungarian, and one is reminded of A. Alvarez's comment that 'With *Crow*, Hughes joins the select band of survivor poets whose work is adequate to the destructive reality we inhabit.' In any event, János Csokits was able to mediate successfully between them. Pilinszky's linguistic 'poverty', as he called it, was surely a factor in Hughes's search for an elemental language, apparent in his translation, for instance, of Seneca's *Oedipus*, or the broken cycle of poems which make up the saga of *Crow*.

Hughes, as has been noted, wrote little about his translations, but he did contribute a short piece about his collaboration with Csokits in translating poems by Pilinszky (see Hughes, 'Postscript to János Csokits' Note', *Translating Poetry: The Double Labyrinth*, 1989). Hughes came to the conclusion that absolute faithfulness to the literal version of the original was called for. He saw himself, as he put it, as the 'troubled mechanic', rather than Csokits's 'co-pilot'. He concludes: 'I am certain I would never have become as interested in Pilinszky as I eventually did, if my curiosity had not been caught in the first place by Csokits' swift word-for-word translations from the page at odd times during our long friendship. [. . .] But even more exciting, for me, was the knack he had of projecting a raw, fresh sense of the strange original – the particular and to me alien uniqueness of the original.' He further stresses the point, making a case for literal translation, as he saw it, at least in this case: 'Faithfulness to the original is crucial in translating Pilinszky's poetry. [. . .] The sense of selfless, courageous testimony pushed to a near-saintly pitch is very strong in Pilinszky. It puts a translator under exacting obligations. There is no question of introducing anything from the translator's own poetical medicine bag.'

In his introductory essay to the selection they translated, Hughes had originally wanted to illustrate his indebtedness to Csokits by including Csokits's literal, annotated version of Pilinszky's 'ultimate statement', 'Apocrypha'. But, as he put it, 'in the end my version inched itself so close to his that there would be no point now in printing two almost identical texts.' The selection below is from *János Pilinszky: The Desert of Love* (1989), translated by János Csokits and Ted Hughes; a revised edition, *The Desert of Love*, was published in 1989. Appendix 8 includes an excerpt from Hughes's Introduction to the *Selected Poems* and part of János Csokits's literal translation of 'The French Prisoner'.

Harbach 1944

to Gábor Thurzó

At all times I see them.
The moon brilliant. A black shaft looms up.
Beneath it, harnessed men
haul a huge cart.

Dragging that giant wagon
which grows bigger as the night grows
their bodies are divided among
the dust, their hunger and their trembling.

They are carrying the road, they are carrying the land,
the bleak potato fields,
and all they know is the weight of everything,
the burden of the skylines

and the falling bodies of their companions
which almost grow into their own
as they lurch, living layers,
treading each other's footsteps.

The villages stay clear of them,
the gateways withdraw.
The distance, that has come to meet them,
reels away back.

Staggering, they wade knee deep
in the low, darkly muffled clatter
of their wooden clogs
as through invisible leaf litter.

Already their bodies belong to silence.
And they thrust their faces towards the height
as if they strained for a scent
of the far-off celestial troughs

because, prepared for their coming
like an opened stock-yard,
its gates flung savagely back,
death gapes to its hinges.

The French Prisoner

If only I could forget that Frenchman.
I saw him, a little before dawn, creeping past our hut
into the dense growth of the back garden
so that he almost merged into the ground.
As I watched he looked back, he peered all round –
at last he had found a safe hideout.
Now his plunder can be all his!
Whatever happens, he'll go no further.

And already he is eating, biting into the turnip
which he must have smuggled out under his rags.
He was gulping raw cattle-turnip!
Yet he had hardly swallowed one mouthful
before it vomited back up.
Then the sweet pulp in his mouth mingled
with joy and revulsion the same
as the happy and unhappy are coupled
in their bodies' ravenous ecstasy.

Only to forget that body, those convulsed shoulder blades,
the hands shrunk to bone,
the bare palm that crammed at his mouth, and clung there
so that it ate, too.
And the shame, desperate, furious,
of the organs savaging each other,
forced to tear from each other
their last shreds of kinship.

The way his clumsy feet had been left out
of the gibbering, bestial elation –
and splayed there, squashed beneath
the torture and rapture of his body.
And his glance – if only I could forget that!
Though he was choking, he kept on
forcing more down his gullet – no matter what –
only to eat – anything – this – that – even himself!

Why go on. Guards came for him.
He had escaped from the nearby prison camp.

And just as I did then, in that garden,
I am strolling here, among garden shadows, at home.
I look into my notes and quote:
'If only I could forget that Frenchman . . .'
And from my ears, from my eyes, my mouth
the scorching memory roars at me:

'I am hungry!' And suddenly I feel
the everlasting hunger
that poor creature has long since forgotten
and which no earthly nourishment can lessen.
He lives on me. And more and more hungrily!
And I am less and less sufficient for him.
And now he, who would have eaten anything,
is yelling for my heart.

On the Wall of a KZ-Lager

Where you have fallen, you stay.
In the whole universe, this is your place.
Just this single spot.
But you have made this yours utterly.

The countryside evades you.
House, mill, poplar,
each thing strives to be free of you
as if it were mutating in nothingness.

But now it is you who stay.
Did we blind you? You continue to watch us.
Did we rob you? You enriched yourself.
Speechless, speechless, you testify against us.

Passion of Ravensbrück

He steps out from the others.
He stands in the square silence.
The prison garb, the convict's skull
blink like a projection.

He is horribly alone.
His pores are visible.
Everything about him is so gigantic,
everything is so tiny.

And this is all.
                    The rest –
the rest was simply
that he forgot to cry out
before he collapsed.

Impromptu

For months now, I have been wandering
aimlessly. Endlessly.
A sweet deadly sunstroke
tortures and blinds me, night and day.

Where do these visitations come from?
Somebody steps from the water
dazzling, young,
slips through the abrupt darkness.

Her smile lifts toward the shore.
Far off, a few sails blaze.
The vertical noon heat
showers down on the litter of bathing huts.

Details and trivia.
A single flower in the soft wind
turning over and over, as in the fingers
of a mute and wondering baby.

And the melodies. Through all those rooms
the same wash of melodies,
as though the barefoot sea were roaming
among their walls.

But most beautiful of all – the lovers!
their manes glowing out of the shadows
the last beautiful tent of their modesty.

The lovers. And the twilight.
The rows of houses, sinking into the dark.
And over the houses, on the sand,
a tower's ponderous mass.

Who could have dreamed up anything so sad.

The Desert of Love

A bridge, and a hot concrete road –
the day is emptying its pockets,
laying out, one by one, all its possessions.
You are quite alone in the catatonic twilight.

A landscape like the bed of a wrinkled pit,
with glowing scars, a darkness which dazzles.
Dust thickens. I stand numb with brightness
blinded by the sun. This summer will not leave me.

Summer. And the flashing heat.
The chickens stand, like burning cherubs,
in the boarded-up, splintered cages.
I know their wings do not even tremble.

Do you still remember? First there was the wind.
And then the earth. Then the cage.
Flames, dung. And now and again
a few wing-flutters, a few empty reflexes.

And thirst. I asked for water.
Even today I hear that feverish gulping,
and helplessly, like a stone, bear
and quench the mirages.

Years are passing. And years. And hope
is like a tin-cup toppled into the straw.

Unfinished Past

to Ted Hughes

It arrives, it stiffens
on the ashen silent wall:
the moon. A single immense blow.
Its core is a death-stillness.

It shatters the roads
the moonlight shatters them.
It rips the wall apart.
White gushes over the black.

The black day splits with lightning.
And lightning. And lightning.
Cataracts of white and black.
You comb your hair in the magnetic tempest.

You comb your hair in the flashing silence.
In a mirror more vigilant than the unfinished past.

You comb your hair in the mirror
silently, as in a coffin of glass.

Van Gogh

1
They undressed in the dark.
They lay down, they fell asleep.
While you, in the glare,
wept and pondered.

2
Night was falling.
In the ramshackle heat
the sun came paper close.
Everything stopped.
A ball of iron also stood there.

3
'Lamb of the world, lupus in fabula,
I am burning
in the glass cabinet of the present tense.'

The Passion

Only the warmth of the slaughter-house,
its geranium pungency, its soft shellac,
only the sun exists.

In a glass-cased silence
the butcher-boys wash down. Yet what has happened
somehow cannot even now finish.

The Prayer of Van Gogh

The battle lost in the field.
The air held by invaders.
Birds, the sun, and again birds.
By night what will be left of me?

At night only the row of lamps
the yellow wall of dry mud
and from the bottom of the garden, through trees,
like a row of candles, the windows,

where I too dwelt and do not dwell,
the house where I lived and do not live,
the roof which tucked me in safely.
Ah God, then you covered me up safely.

Marin Sorescu

Marin Sorescu (1936–96) was one of the most popular and widely translated poets of 'the other Europe' and a frequent visitor to poetry festivals in Western Europe and elsewhere. Born into a peasant family, he wrote in a grimly humorous fashion, implicitly critical of the political status quo in his country, Romania, but also of the human condition in general. While he published widely, he also wrote 'secret poems' which could not be published at the time (see *Censored Poems*, translated by John Hartley Williams and Hilde Ottschofski, 2001). Other books by Sorescu that have appeared in translation are: *Selected Poems* (1983), covering the years 1965–73; *Let's Talk about the Weather* (1985); *The Thirst of the Salt Mountain* (1985); *Dracula the Impaler* (1987); and *The Bridge* (2001). After the fall of Communism, Sorescu was made Minister of Culture. The selection below is from *The Biggest Egg in the World* (Bloodaxe, 1987), to which Ted Hughes contributed along with a number of other English-language poets. Joanna Russell-Gebbett, a Romanian friend of Sorescu's, with her husband, supplied the publisher with the literal versions on the basis of which the English poets produced their translations.

Hughes's comments, in a letter (12 July 1986) to Edna Longley, who supervised the project, indicate his intention to remain as close to the literal meaning as is grammatically and syntactically possible: 'The literals you sent seem to me often just right. In several of these I've barely altered more than a word or two, as you'll see. I must say, my own feeling about translation is that I'm more and more interested in simply the literal crib, with all its oddities.' As is shown by his reworking of the literal text of 'The Whistle' (see Appendix 9), this perennial intention is not always to be taken literally; nevertheless, it was clearly crucial for him to feel he was in close, physical contact with the source text and not merely glossing or lending it a particular dazzle.

Ballad

> When lovers have caught fire all over
> They hold hands
> And throw themselves

Into a wedding ring
With a little water in it.

It's an important fall in life
And they smile happily
And have their arms full of flowers
And they slide very tenderly
And they slide majestically on foot,
Calling out each other's name in the daytime
And hearing themselves at night.

After a while
Their days and nights get mixed up
In a sort of thick sadness . . .

The wedding ring answers
From the other world.
Over there
Is a big beach
Covered with bones
Which embrace
And sleep in their exhausted whiteness
Like beautiful shells
Which loved each other all their sea.

The Whistle

Suddenly a whistle
Shrieks out
Behind a passer-by

Whose body fills instantly with sawdust
Like a tree when it feels
At the edge of the forest
The saw

Even so, says the man to himself, let's not look round –
Maybe it's for somebody else.
Anyway, let's have a respite
Of a few more steps.

The whistle shrieks
Piercing
Again and again
Behind every passer-by

They turn purple, yellow, green, red
And go on walking, stiffened,
Without turning their heads.
Maybe it's for somebody else –
Each one is thinking –
What have I done, only
One war, two wars?
And tomorrow I've the wedding
And the day after tomorrow my wife will give birth
In two days' time I bury my parents –
I've so much to do, so many things.
It can't be for me.

A child
Bought himself a whistle
And went out to try it
On the boulevard
Blowing it impishly in people's ears.

Group

They'd been living together for a long time
And were beginning to repeat each other:
He was her
And she was him,
She was her
And he was her as well,
She was, she wasn't,
And he was them,
Or something like that.

Especially in the morning,
Until they'd sorted out
Who was who,

From where to where,
Why this way and not that,
A lot of time elapsed,
Time poured away like water.

Occasionally they wanted to kiss each other
But realised, at some point,
That they were both her –
Easier just to repeat.

Then they'd start yawning with fear,
A yawn like soft wool,
Which could even be crocheted
This way:
One was yawning very carefully
The other was holding the ball.

Camillo Pennati

Camillo Pennati was born in Milan in 1931. He lived in London from 1958 to 1970, working for the Italian Cultural Institute. From 1973 to 1987, he was an editor with Einaudi in Turin. Pennati has published many collections of poetry and has also translated work by three English poets, Thom Gunn, Philip Larkin and Ted Hughes. Hughes's notebooks contain several draft translations of poems by Pennati, who made a selection himself of poems he thought 'less complicated to render into English', providing Hughes with literals. A collection, containing originals and Hughes's translations, was published in Italy, in 1990 (*Gabbiano e altri versi / On Edge*).

Pennati wrote 'Seascape' originally in English. Appendix 10 contains the English source text, together with Hughes's version of this. Pennati's Italian translation of his own English source text is appended since, uniquely, Hughes made use of this as well. Appended also is an excerpt from a letter from Hughes to Pennati in which he expresses his familiar preference for what he saw as the 'literal'. He seems to have been quite pleased with the results, though with reservations; it is also evident that he felt that what the two of them had managed to do was about as much as a translation could do, insofar as the particular qualities of the original 'cannot be imposed on a given chunk of language – as a translator can only impose. They can only be exuded with the original expression from the original mind.'

Seascape

> Waves into waves their streaming manes
> unfolding seas
> of immemorial time driving the rain
> from the twist of clouds foggy or stormy
> till air from the turmoil that blinds it
> clears to a silken gaze
> quivering on a limitless iris of colours
> deep on reflecting elements of thick depths
> now that the heaving swell subsides

to a breathing lull to flexing scales
and the lathered cress to riding glitters
sparkling vivacity of light
like uppermost leaves of forests
though made of water over its fluid reaches of streaming
green or blue far as the eye goes
or brimming where land falls
dizzily or gently within the attraction
and the atmospheric
gravity of down to earth existence
continuing as time conducts so many
shapes of life to so many
shapes of startled beauty reflecting
with the insight of light all their embraces
that quiver into shadows where
they breathe and share space
leafing through their volume
into an illuminated page of time.

Gull

Master of the sense of emptiness
and of the sense of fullness
master of storms
and calms in the air's
moving element to which you entrust yourself
as you hover
above the shore far up
over the sheer vertigo of your choice
between what fluctuates with dark silvery blades
and the abrupt fixity of rock
between the unencumbered space
extending its reflection over airy layers
and the unmoving hold of the overnight places
before and within and beyond the growing of time
into what, lasting through a material form,
is consumed by its own endurance:
fleeing and encompassing with your gaze

keeled and winged
in a twin buoyancy in the quick and agile
design of existence
which in its own antithesis embodies
the timeless instant
of desire grasped and enacted
in your sensuous flight
crossing that realm.

Lorenzo de' Medici

Lorenzo the Magnificent (1449–92) was the most celebrated of the Medici rulers of Florence. Machiavelli called him 'the greatest patron of literature and art that any prince has ever been'. Leonardo da Vinci and Michelangelo worked at his court. Lorenzo had a particular interest in poetry and music and was a major influence in the development of the madrigal. He wrote a great deal of verse, including *laudi*, spiritual songs, and the very different carnival songs, as well as a verse exposition of Ficino's Neo-Platonism. He also composed naturalistic verse and tales of rustic courtship, as well as treatments of classical legends. His work is esteemed on the same level as that of his *quattrocento* contemporaries, masters of the vernacular lyric, such as Angelo Poliziano (also Lorenzo's protégé) and Count Matteo Maria Boiardo.

Ted Hughes's translations of poems by Lorenzo were based on interlinear versions by Gaia Servadio. They were done for a celebration of Lorenzo's poetry at the Academia Italiana (no longer extant) in London. There are typed versions of some eleven poems, six of these being printed below. Gaia Servadio sent Hughes a number of other English versions of Lorenzo's poetry, but Hughes found that although the material was of intrinsic interest – the Medici court was one of the centres of Neo-Platonism and Hermetic learning – he needed versions that were far more exact, as close to word-for-word transcriptions as possible. In a letter to Gaia Servadio, he explained exactly what he had in mind: 'I had a go at the translations yesterday. After some hours, I got a passable version of that longish piece from the altercazione [the verse exposition of Ficino's Neo-Platonism] but remain uncertain about several details. Looking over the rest, I see many many more hours – not many more hours translating but many many more hours simply untangling the versions to correspond with my guessing at the 15th C Italian, or even at the plain Italian, of the original. If you could let me have an absolutely literal version – as primitive as you please, but literal (the more word by word literal the better) I fancy I could do it pretty quickly.'

Servadio read the poems to Hughes in Italian and later he urged her to let him know if anything worried her in his translations. She commented on the difficulty of dealing with the many allusions to Dante. She recalls, incidentally, that she also tried to interest Hughes in translating poems by Michelangelo, who had compared writing poetry to carving stone.

See Appendix 11 for a note by Servadio on her collaboration with Hughes and the presentation at the Academia Italiana where she was in charge of a series of literary programmes. Her interlinear version of the first poem presented below, Sonetto IX ('How futile every hope is, that we have'), is also appended.

'How futile every hope is, that we have'

How futile every hope is, that we have,
How illusory, all our designs,
And how crammed this world with ignorance,
We learn from our master – the Grave.

Some think singing and dancing and parties are life,
Some let quieter matters guide their minds,
Some detest the world and its substances,
Some live a secret they show nothing of.

Vain worries and thoughts, and diverse fates
For the whole variety of creation,
Find us, each time, straying over the earth.

Each thing has a moment – that flits,
For Fortune's a sickness of perpetual motion.
Nothing is still. And nothing lasts. Only death.

'Alas, during this carnival'

Alas, during this carnival
We women have mislaid
The six husbands we had.
Without them, things look bad.

We all come from Arcetri.
We work in the orchards there.
We grow a peculiar
Fruit fine as our country.

O give a kindly thought –
Bring us to our men.

These fruits will be yours, then.
They are sweet, they do not hurt.

We have huge cucumbers –
Their skins seem to be studded,
Just like warts, all rough and odd,
But they are hearty and wholesome.

You can take them in both hands.
Peel aside a bit of rind,
Open your mouth and then suck hard –
You'll soon find, it does not hurt.

A watermelon too, as fat
As a pumpkin, among others.
We keep these for the seed
So more can be born
To make the tongue blood-red
Wings on its feet, like a dragon,
Fierce and beautiful to look at
Scary, but it cannot hurt.

And look we have long beans
For the gourment, so tender.
Also these that are bent
Hard and big, and good cooked hot
With oil, inside a roll.
You hold on to the bottom
And ply up and down with it –
It threatens, but can't hurt.

They say these fruits of ours
Should be eaten after dinner.
To us – that sounds mad.
To digest them is tough.
A body full of dinner
We call full enough.
And yet, before or after, do
Just as you please, it's up to you.
But try them before, they're not at all bad.

These fruits that are so good –
If you'll point out our husbands –
They're yours, and free for all.
You see we are fresh and young.
If you've no gratitude
We'll find some other ready hand
To help us plough our bit of land
Here at the carnival.

'Less and less fearful, more and more beautiful'

Less and less fearful, more and more beautiful,
Love revealed my adored enemy –
As the thoughts of the day and weariness
Sank into a lazy drowse in the evening.

Shown to my eyes exactly as she is
Only without her usual hard manner,
And wide open to all the loving rays –
Never had any truth seemed so truthful.

Fearful and slow, before I spoke,
I was as I always am. Till dread
Overcame desire, and I began:

'My lady' – and at that, like a wind, she was gone.
In the same instant she snatched from me
My sleep, herself and my very soul, as she fled.

'So who is that man there, with ruddy cheeks'

So who is that man there, with ruddy cheeks,
And two together with him in long cloaks?
And he: 'These three are grave ecclesiastics.

The fattest is the rector of Antella
And so that all might think how well he looks
He always keeps cosmetics in his wallet.

That other, whose sweet laughter you hear ripple,
The one/He with the nose so pointed, long and strange,
Has likewise made himself quite comfortable –

His dignity, as Priest of Fiesole,
Being also devoted to the cup
Which Sir Antonio, his curate, fills

In every corner and at every season
Always that loyal vessel's close to hand.
I say no more, before the procession.

But I think he was always his escort.
When he shifts town for town, and court for court,
This is the one that/who taps upon his door.

So this/And will be there beside him, after/at his death
And should be placed beside him in his tomb
To comfort both his carcase and his wraith.

This will be his bequest/last will. Have you seen
When, during the procession, a command
Brings them all to a halt? And how then,

When his brothers, at the superior's call,
Make their circle together, have you seen,
While their lifted cassocks cover/undo them all

How he covers his face – with his cup?'

'The tiny ant'

The tiny ant
Brings the sun's flame, burning and clear,
Out of the ancient caves.
The sage, who learns instantly
Then tells the others
Where the mean peasant cunningly hid
A small mound of grain.
So out hurries the black, possessive horde,
One by one

They come to the pile, and they go.
They carry the plundered bounty
In mouths and in hands.
They arrive eager and light,
Heavy and loaded they go.
They block the narrow path,
And collide. While one sets down his burden
The other gives him the news
Of the new booty, more attractive,
And so to the delicious labour
Always invites him.
Trodden and thick and laboured is the long track.
If each one comes with something,
Dearer, and always more cherished,
As it should be, is the thing
Without which there can be no life.
The stolen load is light
If the tiny animal dies without it.
So my thoughts
Scamper lightly to my fine woman,
Bump against hers coming to me.
They stop and confer.
Sweet is the prey
If they bring, as the ants do,
Anything at all to the precious
Immortal store.

'As if to have taken my freedom were not enough'

As if to have taken my freedom were not enough,*
And to have wrenched me from the chaste path
Without yet wanting my death,
In such pain and so new to my life,

You left me without a thought
That when you left me, strengthless and pale

---

* A woman is speaking here, pleading, complaining. [note by GS]

(A true sign that my end would be early)
I remained, hating my own beauty.

Nor can I think of anything but those times
That were the cause of my gentle/soft weeping,
My sweet martyrdom, my sad contentment.

If the remembrance were not still one means
Of consoling tortured lovers
I would have ended all this grief with death.

Ovid

Publius Ovidius Naso (43 BC–AD 18) was one of the most prolific poets of Rome's Golden Age. Born a year after the murder of Julius Caesar, Ovid went to Rome during Augustus's rule to continue his education, his father intending him for a political career. He rapidly became Rome's most successful poet, until in AD 9 Augustus suddenly dispatched him into exile, to Tomis (modern Constanza, in Romania), the exact circumstances of this disaster remaining unclear. In any case, Ovid wrote some of his finest poetry about exile.

The *Metamorphoses*, his most celebrated work, is the product of his middle years. He regarded it, apparently, as a continuous epic – Ted Hughes's non-observance of this much-praised aspect of the poem has been criticised by Classicists – rather than a collection of myths. The stories are bound together thematically, chronologically, and in many other ways, there being a general movement from gods acting like humans to humans becoming gods. Among readers of the late Middle Ages, the *Metamorphoses* rivalled the Bible in popularity, influencing among many others Chaucer, Spenser, Shakespeare and Milton. It is from Ovid's *Metamorphoses* and his *Fasti* (a poetical calendar of the Roman year) that we take most of our stories of Greek and Roman mythology.

Hughes was the most prolific contributor (four long sections) to *After Ovid: New Metamorphoses*, edited by Michael Hofmann and James Lasdun (Faber, 1994), who were assembling a collection of translations of episodes from the *Metamorphoses*, commissioning a number of American and British contemporary poets. Hofmann and Lasdun allowed almost total latitude; in their Introduction to *After Ovid* (in which they quote Miller), they describe how 'we invited each contributor to translate, reinterpret, reflect on or completely reimagine the narrative. [. . .] Without prescribing how, we wanted an Ovid remade, made new.' They continue: 'By definition it resisted close control. Along the way we decided . . . to divide the book into self-contained narrative sections of anything from ten lines to ten pages; and to dispense with Ovid's division of the whole into individual books, while preserving his general running order as far as possible.' They were of course aware that in so doing they were disrupting the seamlessness of Ovid's narrative, but decided to 'loosen these bonds' in the interest, presumably, of freedom for the contributing poets and in the belief that readers would make connections for themselves. There was some disappointment among Classicists that the connections between the stories were no longer explicit, as a result of this organisation of the work, but there were gains as well, not least the fact that its openness encouraged Hughes, for one, to continue translating Ovid.

Hughes completed a substantial part of the *Metamorphoses* (in twenty-four parts), and his *Tales from Ovid* (Faber, 1997) is surely among his major works. Hughes ends his short introduction to *Tales from Ovid* rather chillingly: 'They establish a rough register of what it feels like to live in the psychological gulf that opens at the end of an era. Among everything else that we see in them, we certainly recognize this.' However, he vouchsafes nothing about his procedure as a translator. It seems that he made use of Arthur Golding's celebrated translation of 1567, characterised by Ezra Pound as 'the most beautiful book in the English language' (Pound, 'Notes on Elizabethan Classicists', 1917), and the Latin source text, with the accompanying literal translation (Loeb Classics, first published 1916) by Frank Justus Miller to help him out with the Latin. (Miller was also the translator of Seneca's *Oedipus*, this being the text Peter Brook initially used in rehearsing the actors for his 1968 National Theatre production.)

Shakespeare drew on the *Metamorphoses* for his long poem 'Venus and Adonis', discussion of which – and of Shakespeare's other long poem, 'The Rape of Lucrece' – is the basis of Hughes's 1971 introduction to *Poems from Shakespeare* (republished as *A Choice of Shakespeare's Verse*, Faber, 1991) and his *Shakespeare and the Goddess of Complete Being* (Faber, 1992). As Hughes explains in his essay-introduction to Shakespeare's verse, the key moment for tragedy shows 'the agonies of an ancient Dionysus in a world of suddenly hardening sceptical intellect and morality'. In 'Venus and Adonis', as he puts it, 'a love goddess – the love goddess – tries to rape Adonis, a severely puritan youth'. The translation was also included in *After Ovid*, as was the following one, 'Salmacis and Hermaphroditus'. So significant are these poems in the context of Hughes's own work that the whole of 'Venus and Adonis' and an excerpt from 'Salmacis and Hermaphroditus' are reprinted here.

Venus and Adonis (and Atalanta)

> A power in the air hears the last prayer
> Of the desperate. Myrrha's prayer to be no part
> Of either her life or her death was heard and was answered.
>
> The earth gripped both her ankles as she prayed.
> Roots forced from beneath her toenails, they burrowed
> Among deep stones to the bedrock. She swayed,

Living statuary on a tree's foundations.
In that moment, her bones became grained wood,
Their marrow pith,

Her blood sap, her arms boughs, her fingers twigs,
Her skin rough bark. And already
The gnarling crust has coffined her swollen womb.

It swarms over her breasts. It warps upwards
Reaching for her eyes as she bows
Eagerly into it, hurrying the burial

Of her face and her hair under thick-webbed bark.
Now all her feeling has gone into wood, with her body.
Yet she weeps,

The warm drops ooze from her rind.
These tears are still treasured.
To this day they are known by her name – Myrrh.

Meanwhile the meaty fruit her father implanted
Has ripened in the bole. Past its term,
It heaves to rive a way out of its mother.

But Myrrh's cramps are clamped in the heart-wood's vice.
Her gagged convulsions cannot leak a murmur.
She cannot cry to heaven for Lucina.

Nevertheless a mother's agony
Strained in the creaking tree and her tears drench it.
For pity, heaven's midwife Lucina,

Lays her hands on the boughs in their torment
As she recites the necessary magic.
The trunk erupts, the bark splits, and there tumbles

Out into the world with a shattering yell
The baby Adonis. Nymphs of the flowing waters
Cradle him in grasses. They wash him

With his mother's tears. Bittermost envy
Could only glorify such a creature.
A painter's naked Cupid to perfection –

The god's portrait without his arrow quiver
Or his bow. Here, subtlest of things,
Too swift for the human eye, time slips past.

And this miraculous baby of his sister,
Sired by his grandpa, just now born of a bush,
Barely a boy, in the blink of an eye is a man

Suddenly more beautiful than ever –
So beautiful the great Venus herself,
Hovering over the wonder, feels awe.

Then the boy's mother, pent by Venus
In that shrub of shame, finds her revenge.
The goddess falls helplessly for Adonis.

Venus plucking kisses from her Cupid
Snagged her nipple on an unnoticed arrow
Sticking from his quiver. She pushed him away –

But was wounded far worse than she feared.
Pierced by the mortal beauty of Adonis
She has forgotten Cythera's flowery island,

Forgotten the bright beaches of Paphos,
Forgotten Cnidos, delicate as its fish,
Amathus, veined with costly metals. Neglected

Even Olympus. She abstains from heaven
Besotted by the body of Adonis.
Wherever he goes, clinging to him she goes.

She who had loved equally the shade
And her indolence in it, who had laboured
Only as a lily of the valley,

Now goes bounding over the stark ridges,
Skirts tucked high like the huntress, or she plunges
Down through brambly goyles, bawling at hounds,

Hunting the harmless, the hare who sees best backwards,
Hinds with painful eyes like ballerinas,
Tall stags on their dignity. She has nothing

To do with fatal boars. She shuns wolves,
Their back teeth always aching to crack big bones.
Bears with a swipe like a dungfork. Lions,

Lank bellies everlastingly empty,
That lob over high bomas, as if weightless,
With bullocks in their jaws. 'These,' she cried,

'O my beloved, are your malefic planets.
Never hesitate to crush a coward
But, challenged by the brave, conceal your courage.

'Leave being bold many love, to the uglier beasts.
Else you stake my heart in a fool's gamble.
Let Nature's heavier criminals doze on

'Or you may win your glory at my cost.
The beauty, the youth, the charms that humbled Venus,
Feel silly and go blank when suddenly a lion

'Looks their way. They have no influence
On whatever lifts a boar's bristles,
Or on the interests or on the affections

'Of any of that gang. The tusk of the boar
Is the lightning jag that delivers the bolt.
The ignorant impact of solidified

'Hunger in the arrival of a lion
Turns everything to dust. I abhor them!'

'But why should you abhor them?'
    'There is a lesson

'These coarse brutes can teach us. But first,
This hunter's toil is more than my limbs are used to.
Look, that kindly poplar has made cool

'A bed of shade in the grass, just for us.'
So Venus pillowed her head on the chest of Adonis.
Then, to her soft accompaniment of kisses:

    'Once the greatest runner was a woman – so swift
    She outran every man.

It is true. She could and she did.
But none could say which was more wonderful –
The swiftness of her feet or her beauty.

'When this woman questioned the oracle
About her future husband
The god said: "Atalanta,
Stay clear of a husband.
Marriage is not for you. Nevertheless

' "You are fated to marry.
And therefore fated, sooner or later, to live
Yourself but other." The poor girl,
Pondering this riddle, alarmed,
Alerted, alone in a thick wood,

'Stayed unmarried.
The suitors who kept at her stubbornly
She met
With a fearful deterrent:
"You can win me," she told them,

' "Only if you can outrun me.
That is to say, if you will race against me.
Whoever wins that race – he is my husband.
Whoever loses it – has lost his life.
This is the rule for all who dare court me."

'Truly she had no pity.
But the very ferocity
Of this grim condition of hers
Only lent her beauty headier power –
Only made her suitors giddier.

'Hippomenes watched the race.
"What fool," he laughed, "would wager life itself
Simply to win a woman –
With a foregone conclusion against him?
This is a scheme to rid the world of idiots."

'But even as he spoke he saw the face
Of Atalanta. Then as her dress opened

And fell to her feet
He saw her dazzling body suddenly bared.
A beauty, O Adonis, resembling mine

'Or as yours would be if you were a woman.
Hippomenes' brain seemed to turn over. His arms
As if grabbing to save himself as he slipped,
Were reaching towards her, fingers hooked,
And he heard his own voice
Coming like somebody else's. "What am I saying?

' "I did not know, I never guessed
What a trophy
You run for –"
And there, as he stammered and stared,
His own heart was lost.

'Suddenly he was terrified of a winner.
He prayed that all would fail and be executed.
"But why," he muttered, "am I not out among them
Taking my chance?
Heaven helps those who give it something to help."

'These words were still whirling in his head
As her legs blurred past him.
Though her velocity was an arrow
As from a Turkish bow of horn and sinew
The shock-wave was her beauty.

'Her running redoubled her beauty.
The ribbon-ties at her ankles
Were the wing-tips of swallows.
The ribbon-ties at her knees
Were the wing-tips of swifts.

'Her hair blazed above her oiled shoulders.
And the flush on her slender body
Was ivory tinted
By rays that glow
Through a crimson curtain,

'And while this hero gazed with drying mouth
It was over.

Atalanta stood adjusting her victor's chaplet
And her defeated suitors, under the knife,
Sprawled as they coughed up her bloody winnings.

'Hippomenes ignored the draining corpses.
He stepped forward – his eyes gripping hers.
"Why do you scry for fame, Atalanta,
In the entrails
Of such pathetic weaklings?

' "Why not run against me?
If I win
You will not be shamed – only surpassed
By the son of Megareus, who was sired by Onchestius,
Who was sired by Neptune, god of the sea.

' "I am Hippomenes –
A great-grandson of the god of the oceans.
I have not disappointed expectations.
If my luck fails, by the fame of Hippomenes
Your fame shall be that much more resplendent."

'Atalanta was astonished as she felt
Her heart falter. Her legs began to tremble.
Her wild rage to conquer seemed to have kneeled
In a prayer to be conquered.
She murmured:

' "Which god, jealous of beautiful youth,
Plots now to slay this one?
Putting it into his head to fling away life.
As I am the judge:
Atalanta is not worth it.

' "It is not his beauty that makes me afraid
Though it well might.
It is his innocence, his boyishness
Touches me, and hurts me.
He is hardly a boy. He is a child.

' "Yet with perfect courage,
Contemptuous of death.

Also fourth in descent, as he claims, from the sea-god.
Also he loves me
And is ready to die if he cannot have me.

' "Listen, stranger,
Get as far away from me as you can
By the shortest route.
Marriage with me is death.
Go while you can move.

' "My bridal bed, my virgin bed, is a sump
Under the executioner's block.
Go and go quickly.
No other woman will refuse you.
The wisest will do all she can to win you.

' "Yet why should I bother myself?
After so gladly killing so many
Why should I care now? Die if you must.
If these poor corpses here cannot deter you,
If you are so sick of your life – then die.

' "They will say: because he dared to love her
She killed him. I shall have to hear:
Her thanks for his fearless love was a shameful death.
This will bring me fame – but ill-fame.
Yet none of it is my fault.

' "You cannot win, Hippomenes,
Forget me.
If only your insanity could shrink
Into your feet as a superhuman swiftness!
Look at him. His face is like a girl's.

' "In me there sleeps evil for both of us.
Do not wake it up. Go quietly away.
You belong to life. But believe me,
If Fate had not made my favour lethal
You alone would be my choice."

'Atalanta knew nothing about love
So she failed

To recognise love's inebriation
As it borrowed her tongue to pronounce these words.
She was hardly aware of what they meant.

'But her father, and the crowd, demanded the race.
And Hippomenes was already praying: "O Venus,
You gave me this great love – now let me keep it."
A quirk of air brought his prayer to my hearing.
Moved, I moved quickly.

'The most precious acre in Cyprus
Is my temple's orchard. A tree grows there
Of solid gold. With leaves of green gold
On boughs of white gold. Among those leaves
Hang apples of red gold. I picked three.

'Visible only to Hippomenes
I taught him the use of these apples.
Then at a blast from the trumpets
Both shot from their marks.
Their feet flickered away and the dust hung.

'They could have been half-flying over water
Just marring the shine.
Or over the silky nape of a field of barley.
Hippomenes felt the crowd's roar lifting him on:
"Hippomenes! You can win! Hippomenes!"

'And maybe Atalanta
Was happier than he was to hear that shout
As she leaned back on her hips, reining back
The terrible bolt of speed in her dainty body,
And clung to him with her glance even as she left him

'Tottering as if to a halt, labouring for air
That scorched his mouth and torched his lungs,
With most of the course to go. This was the moment
For flinging one of my apples out past her –
He bounced it in front of her feet and away to the left.

'Startled to see such a gorgeous trinket
Simply tossed aside, she could not resist it.

While she veered to snatch it up
Hippomenes was ahead, breasting the crest
Of the crowd's roar.

'But Atalanta came back in with a vengeance.
She passed him so lightly he felt to be stumbling.
Out went the second apple.
As if this were as easy she swirled and caught it
Out of a cloud of dust and again came past him.

'Now he could see the flutter of the crowd at the finish.
"O Venus," he sobbed, "let me have the whole of your
    gift!"
Then with all his might he hurled
The last apple
Past and beyond her – into a gulley

'Choked with tumbled rock and thorn. She glimpsed it
Vanishing into a waste
Of obstacles and lost seconds.
With two gold apples heavier at each stride
And the finish so near, she tried to ignore it.

'But I forced her to follow. And the moment she found it
That third apple I made even heavier.
Lugging her three gold prizes far behind
Her race was lost. Atalanta belonged to the winner.
So their story begins.

'But tell me, Adonis, should he have given me thanks
And burned costly perfumes in my honour?
Neither thanks nor perfumes arrived. He forgot my help.

'Anger overtook me. I was hurt.
I swore I would never again be slighted so.
My revenge would scare mankind for ever.

'Now hear the end of the story. This fine pair
Worn out with their wanderings, in a deep wood
Found a temple
Built long since for Cybele, Mother of the Gods,
Whose face is a black meteorite.

'Both thought they were tired enough that night
to sleep on the stone paving. Till I kissed
The ear of Hippomenes
With a whisper. As my lips touched him he shivered
Into a fit of lust like epilepsy.

'Under the temple was a cave shrine
Hollowed in solid bedrock and far older
Than the human race. An unlit crypt.
It was walled
With wooden images of the ancient gods.

'This was the sanctum doomed Hippomenes
Now defiled,
Sating himself on the body of Atalanta.
The desecrated wooden images
Averted their carved faces in horror.

'And the tower-crowned Mother of All, Cybele,
Considered plunging both
As they copulated
Into Styx, the tarpit of bubbling hell.
But that seemed insufficient to her.

'Instead she dropped maned hides
Over their sweating backs. Hardened and hooked
Their clutching fingers into talons. Let
Their panting chest-keels deepen. Let them sweep
The dust with long tails. Gargoyle-faced,

'And now with speech to match, these godless lovers
Rumble snarls, or cough, or grunt, or roar.
They have the thorny scrub for a nuptial chamber
And are lions – their loathsome fangs obedient
Only to the bridle-bits of Cybele.

'O dear love,
These and the others like them, that disdain
To give your hounds a run but come out looking for the
    hunter,
For my sake, O dear boy, let them lie.
Do not ruin our love with your recklessness.'

Her lesson done, the goddess climbed with her swans
Towards lit clouds. Meanwhile, as Adonis
Pondered her parable to find a meaning,

His hounds woke a wild boar in a wallow.
When this thug burst out his boar-spear's point
Glanced off the bone into the hump of muscle.

The boar deftly hooked the futile weapon
Out of the wound and turned on the hunter,
Overtook the boy's panic scramble,

Bedded its dagger tusks in under his crotch
Then ploughed him with all its strength as if unearthing
A tough tree's roots, till it hurled him aside, mangled.

Venus, afloat on swansdown in the high blue,
Still far short of Paphos, felt the shock-wave
Of the death-agony of Adonis.

She banked and diving steeply down through cirrus
Sighted her darling boy where he sprawled
Wallowing in a mire of gluey scarlet.

She leapt to the earth, ripping her garment open.
She clawed her hair and gouged her breasts with her nails,
Pressing her wounds to his wounds as she clasped him

And screaming at the Fates: 'You hags shall not
Have it all your way. O Adonis,
Your monument shall stand as long as the sun.

'The circling year itself shall be your mourner.
Your blood shall bloom immortal in a flower.
Persephone preserved a girl's life

'And fragrance in pale mint. I shall not do less.'
Into the broken Adonis she now dripped nectar.
His blood began to seethe – as bubbles thickly

Bulge out of hot mud. Within the hour
Where he had lain a flower stood – bright-blooded
As those beads packed in the hard rind

Of a pomegranate. This flower's life is brief.
Its petals cling so weakly, so ready to fall
Under the first light wind that kisses it,

We call it 'windflower'.

from Salmacis and Hermaphroditus

'I've won!' shrieked Salmacis. 'He's mine!'
She could not help herself.
'He's mine!' she laughed, and with a couple of bounds
Hit the pool stark naked
In a rocking crash and thump of water –
The slips of her raiment settling wherever
They happened to fall. Then out of the upheaval
Her arms reach and wind round him,
And slippery as the roots of big lilies
But far stronger, her legs below wind round him.
He flounders and goes under. All his strength
Fighting to get back up through a cloud of bubbles
Leaving him helpless to her burrowing kisses.
Burning for air, he can do nothing
As her hands hunt over him, and as her body
Knots itself every way around him
Like a sinewy otter
Hunting some kind of fish
That flees hither and thither inside him,
And as she flings and locks her coils
Around him like a snake
Around the neck and legs and wings of an eagle
That is trying to fly off with it,
And like ivy which first binds the branches
In its meshes, then pulls the whole tree down,
And as the octopus –
A tangle of constrictors, nippled with suckers,
That drag towards a maw –
Embraces its prey.

Frank Wedekind

Frank Wedekind (1861–1918), journalist, circus proprietor, theatrical impresario, cabaret performer and actor, wrote a number of influential, explicit, grotesque tragi-comedies, castigating the hypocrisy of bourgeois morality. In *Spring Awakening* (1891) he takes on the decaying and repressive educational system, not long before everything comes apart anyway in the First World War. The play was not staged until 1906, and was first performed in England in 1963; a translation by Edward and Elisabeth Bond-Pablé was staged in 1974. Wedekind was greatly admired by Brecht as well, who followed him in combining various theatrical elements – dialogue, music, gesture, folklore and the poetic – with realism.

Ted Hughes's new translation of *Spring Awakening (Frühlings Erwachen)*, written at the invitation of Tim Supple, was first performed by the Royal Shakespeare Company at the Pit in the Barbican, London, on 2 August 1995. Hughes had been interested in Supple's adaptation of Carol Ann Duffy's treatment of Grimm's fairytales, which, like Wedekind's play, have both a social and a folk dimension. Supple felt that Hughes might in particular be able to render the 'strange kind of maturity of kids' dialogue . . . the intensity of feeling experienced by children and the proximity to death and eternal powers that are part of life in adolescence'. In the excerpts below, adolescent boys discuss sex and reflect on the repressiveness of the parental world. The naturalness of the dialogue, as rendered by Hughes, contrasts with Wedekind's non-realistic overall treatment.

Excerpt 1
(*Act One, Scene 2. Melchior Gabor meets Moritz Steifel. They try to reconcile social demands and the instinctual.*)

MORITZ
It's suddenly so dark. I can't see my hand in front of my face. Where've you gone? Melchior – don't you believe that man's sense of shame is completely artificial – manufactured by his upbringing?

MELCHIOR

The other day I was thinking about just that. I would say shame is rooted in human nature. You can't escape it. Imagine you're ordered to take all your clothes off in front of your best friend. You wouldn't. Or you'd do it – only if he did exactly the same, at the same time.

MORITZ

If ever I have children they'll all sleep in the same room – right from the start. If possible the same bed. Night and morning they'll help undress and dress each other – boys and girls, all together. In summer, when it's hot, they'll all wear a very simple short tunic – white linen or something of that sort – light and simple. Fastened with leather thongs. Think how those children would grow up – so relaxed and easy with each other. And look at us.

MELCHIOR

You're right, Moritz. I'm sure you are. The only snag is – what happens when the girls get pregnant?

MORITZ

What do you mean? Get pregnant?

MELCHIOR

Instinct, Moritz. That's one thing we have to believe in, like it or not. The instinctive drives. Suppose you shut up a tom-cat and a female cat together, from birth, for life, no other cats near them, never a glimpse of one other cat – nothing in there with them but their own drive. What happens? One day, bang, the female's pregnant. And neither of them ever got a hint how to do it from any other cat. Not one lesson.

Excerpt 2
(*Act Two, Scene 1. Moritz tries to understand female pleasure.*)

MORITZ

. . . The girl's pleasure – girls are like gods in their pleasures. A girl tries to protect herself, doesn't she? It's her instinct to resist. But right up to the very last moment, she suspends any resentment or fear or anger – so all at once she can see the heavens open and engulf her. And that's the moment when she most dreads hell and damnation – as her paradise bursts into flower. All her feelings unspoiled, fresh, astonishing to her – like a spring gushing out of a rock. She lifts a cup – no human lip has ever touched it – a great goblet of nectar, flaming and flickering, and she drains it, gulp after gulp. Well, compared to that, how flat and pitiful must a man's pleasure be.

MELCHIOR
Think whatever you like, but keep it to yourself. I don't even let myself think about it.

Excerpt 3
(*Act Two, Scene 3. One of the boys, Hans Rilow, meditates on the nature of sex, interjecting fragments from* Othello, *and invoking works of art which afford further clues to an understanding of his inchoate feelings.*)

Rilow in lavatory. He lifts toilet seat.

RILOW
Have you prayed tonight, Desdemona?

Takes from under his shirt the Venus of Palma Vecchi.

You don't seem to be praying very hard, my lovely – so deliciously contemplating all that is still to come – Just as in that moment of our first encounter, that wave of rapture when I spied you in the window of Schlesinger's shop – between a brass candlestick and a hunting knife. Those flowering limbs, just as they were then, the swelling soft curve of your hips, those girlish breasts, so eager, so unworldly, not one bit less alluring. How giddy with joy that painter must have been when his fourteen-year-old model lay there lolling across the divan, right in front of his eyes – and he could reach out and touch her.
Will you visit me in my dreams sometimes? I shall rise in

the warm bed, my arms outstretched, and I'll kiss you till you gasp. You shall take possession of me – as the heiress takes possession of her derelict castle, when doors and gates swing open to invisible hands, and down in the park, once more, the fountain begins to jet and splash –

It is the cause, it is the cause –

[. . .]

How many like you have gone this way before you? How many beauties have I grappled with on this brink, in this same struggle? First came Thumann's 'Psyche' – a legacy from the shrivelled-up Mademoiselle Angélique, that old rattlesnake in the paradise of my childhood. Correggio's 'Io'. Lossow's 'Galatea'. Then that 'Amor' by Bouguereau. 'Ada' by J. van Beers – the very 'Ada' I had to abduct from the secret drawer of my father's desk, to add to my harem. And that shuddering, ecstatic 'Leda' by Makart. She fell out from my brother's college notes when I was inspecting his progress. That's six. Six before you who paused here, as you do now, staring into the bowels of hell – about to plunge. Let the fact console you. Don't use that imploring gaze to lash my agonies out of control.

[. . .]

But my conscience will recover. And so will my body. Yes, my vigour will return when you, my voluptuous little she-devil, no longer repose in my red-silk-lined jewel case. I think I'll replace you with the 'Lorelei' of Bodenhausen. Or perhaps with Linger's 'Forsaken Woman'. Then again, I might nestle 'Loni' of Defregger into that sumptuous, secret apartment. Those ladies will soon refresh me. Another three months of your unveiled holy of holies, my darling soul would have melted my brains like a butter pat on a grilled fish. The time has come to separate the bed from the banquet.

[. . .]

My heart clenched in a cramp – Ah! What of it! St. Agnes also died for chastity – in a brothel – and she wasn't half as nude as you are, wrapped in her saintly hair. With a single stroke they swept off her head. One more kiss. Your body is all blossoms. These dainty breasts. These moulded, smooth, torturing knees –

It is the cause, it is the cause, my soul;
Let me not name it to you, you chaste stars!
It is the cause.

He drops the picture into the depths. Closes the toilet lid.

Aeschylus

The Greek tragic poet Aeschylus (c.525–456 BC) took part in the battles resisting the Persian invaders and was present both at Marathon and Salamis, his earliest extant play being *The Persians*. The trilogy the *Oresteia*, the only complete trilogy to survive, appeared in 458 BC. Seven of his approximately eighty plays have survived, among these *Prometheus Bound* (one of the sources of *Orghast*). The Oresteian trilogy comprises the *Agamemnon*, the *Choephori* and the *Eumenides*. Broadly speaking, it is concerned with the aftermath of the Trojan War, engaged in by the brother kings Agamemnon and Menelaus, to reclaim Helen, Menelaus's wife, who had been abducted to Troy by its prince, Paris. In the first play, King Agamemnon returns, victorious, with the prophetess Cassandra, a Trojan princess, as a prospective concubine, only to be slaughtered by his wife Clytemnestra, in revenge for the death of their daughter Iphigenia, sacrificed by Agamemnon in Aulis where his fleet had been becalmed. In the second play, Orestes, the son of Agamemnon and Clytemnestra, returns to Argos and at Apollo's command avenges his father's death by killing his mother. Pursued by the avenging Furies (the Eumenides) on account of this matricide, Orestes, in the last play, is finally vindicated by the court of the Areopagus. An end to the bloody history of the royal family of Argos is envisaged.

In June 1994, the artistic director of the Northcott Theatre, Exeter, John Durnin, invited Hughes to produce an 'imaginative retelling' of Aeschylus' *Oresteia* for production in the autumn/winter 1995 season. Durnin had directed Hughes's version of Seneca's *Oedipus* at the Everyman Theatre, Cheltenham. Hughes evidently made extensive use of the well-known translation by Philip Vellacott (first published by Penguin, 1956), setting aside work already begun on Euripides' *Alcestis* (see below). His version of the *Oresteia* was produced by the National Theatre, directed by Katie Mitchell, in 1999, after Hughes's death. In letters to Leonard Baskin, Hughes comments on his work with the *Oresteia*, suggesting that his first aim was to make it more 'actable' than the many existing versions. In December 1995, again to Baskin, he describes his version as 'streamlined and internalised. I tried to release the howl in every line. (Some only have a whimper.)' Despite the ironical comment in parentheses, one detects here a certain satisfaction with the results of his work. At the very least, as with Ovid, he feels that the work has been useful, although he doesn't state in what way. 'It is good for me,' he affirms in a letter to Baskin. Of the Ovid he had written that it 'is amusing to do. But is it useful – to me?' Translation of these monumental works seems to have been his way of reading these texts, orientating himself among them. His concern, however, is always to produce a text that will live in the present, either in the reader's mind or, especially, on the stage.

In his translation (Faber, 1999), as with Seneca and Racine, Hughes does not attempt to reproduce the metre, but sparely and vividly confronts the myth. In general he exercises much self-restraint, remaining true to his own 'literalistic' aims, and if he takes liberties, these are in deleting rather than adding. While clearly aiming at immediacy, he is mindful of formal considerations (more than a shadow of the Alexandrine lies over his translation of *Phèdre*).

See Appendix 13 for the translation by Philip Vellacott (which is partially rhyming) of the first part of Excerpt 1, below, and a recent more literal scholarly version by Hugh Lloyd-Jones.

Excerpt 1

(Agamemnon *Chorus describes the embarcation for Troy of the Argive fleet under the twin monarchs, Agamemnon and Menelaus, and recounts the ominous killing of a pregnant hare by two birds of prey, representing the two royal brothers.*)

> I am the man to tell this tale.
> Old age
> Takes away everything
> Except a few words the gods have tested,
> For the eye
> That opens towards the grave
> Sees the core of things and is prophetic.
> As our two Kings set out,
> As their floating forest of spears
> Lifted anchor,
> Two birds,
> Hook-beaked, big-winged birds,
> Sailed over
> On the right – on the right!

Good fortune!
The whole army cheered the good omen –
Victory!

Then those two birds,
The black bird and the white bird,
Flushed and drove and killed
A hare heavy with her twins.
The whole army
Saw them kill the pregnant hare. They saw
The black bird and the white bird
That had brought them promise of victory
Rip the mother's womb and drag from it
The living unborn tenants –
The whole army watched from start to finish
That murder of the unborn.
If evil is in this wind, let it blow over.

Calchas the seer
Recognised the birds,
The white bird and the black,
Menelaus and Agamemnon.
Calchas
Cried to the whole army and the two Kings:
'What does this kill mean? I will tell you.
It means
Victory with a twist.
Fate will destroy
All Troy's cattle,
All Troy's crops,
And at last
Will open to you the city's holy of holies.
But when you have emptied Troy of her blood and her
    babies,
Then you can expect the anger of heaven.
Artemis, the moon-faced, the goddess,
The mother of the hares,
Beautiful Artemis,
Deity of the womb and its mystery,
Protectress of mothers and their darlings,

She has heard the death-cry of the hare,
She has seen what her father's birds have done,
She has looked through the bloody spy-hole
Where the hare's womb was plucked out.
She has seen the bigger murder behind it
Still to be committed
By the hooked heads,
The white bird and the black bird –
What will she do now?

Excerpt 2

(*Chorus tells how Agamemnon felt obliged to sacrifice his daughter
Iphigenia, the fleet being prevented by an absence of breeze from
sailing from Aulis.*)

Agamemnon
Heard the terror stirring and looming
Through the words of the seer.
But he was no longer a man in a man's body
Confronting the lonely fate
That would kill him.
He was a war-machine,
A launching campaign, a whole nation of vengeance.
His profile was the prow of a thousand ships.
Meanwhile, the wrong wind had caught our fleet
And pinned us under the lee of Aulis.
Everything followed.
A big sea built off the point.
It was the wall of a prison. In that bay
The whole army lay trapped. The weeks passed.
The rigging of the ships rotted.
And the men fermented. In the squalls
Ships dragged their anchors, gored each other,
Crushed each other's ribs, wrecked each other,
Then broke up in the surf, against rocks.
Stores dwindled and mouldered.
Men's minds started to go.
Explosions of boredom, screaming quarrels.

Senseless killings. Mutinies, desertions,
Feuds between factions. Finally, the sickness.
Under that locked wind
The overcrowded prison that had been an army
Became a hospital.

Excerpt 3
(*Chorus describes the battle with Troy.*)

The gusty wind
On the plains of Troy
Has torn the voices
Out of their chests
And scattered like smoke
The shapes of their faces
And puffed them inland
To cool Helen.

Now throughout Argos
The mourning for the slain
Gathers like a curse.
Rulers should fear,
Above all, one thing:
The gathering curse
Of their own people.

It curdles the daylight
Thick as a darkness –
A fear in the air.
A weight you can feel
and have to bear.

That leader who herds
His people en masse
Into glorious graves –
Let him be sure:
Heaven is watching.
When his high hand
Unbalances justice

The Furies wake up.
That man strides
Assured and proud
Into the abyss.

Excerpt 4
(A herald tells of the suffering of the soldiers.)

Our huge task is done.
All as we wished it.
Yet what did it amount to?
Time scrambles the memory.
Good and evil
Were there in plenty.
The gods can be happy
For a thousand lifetimes.
Suffering belongs
To the days of man.
We suffered in the ships, tortured by boredom and lice,
By the stench, sodden with sweat, vomit, urine –
Sleep a cramp of agony, tumbled in storms –
And on land the dog-holes were worse.
The stench, the rats, the cockroaches, worse.
Filthy with flies and dysentery,
Crutches raw and bleeding, we dug in
Under the enemy's wall. We lived there
Pelted with their ordure,
Or made our beds in the salt marsh
With the crabs and mosquitoes.
Our finger-joints clubbed with rheumatism,
Icy or streaming with fever.
In every ten men, nine were trembling.
Then, God help us, the winter.
The wind off those white peaks.
Toes fell off, birds dropped out of the trees.
A man's back could snap if he bent of a sudden.
Then in midsummer the heat – the heat!
The sea was a puddle of lead.

The earth too hot for the bare footsole.
The touch of bronze blistered.

Excerpt 5
(*Chorus narrates a fable about a lion cub, to show how a man's
essential nature cannot be changed.*)

>A farmer took a lion cub home.
>He let it suckle milk, with the lambs.
>It played with his children, and they cuddled it.
>The grandparents smiled to see the cub
>Romping among the lambs and the children.
>The shepherd nursed the cub in his arms.
>It slept in the crook of his arm, or on his knees.
>The neighbours laughed and thought it wonderful
>To see a lion cub licking the father's face.
>But the lion nature could not be hidden.
>Time passed, and the day of the lion dawned
>Over the farmer's whole family –
>The screams and roars went up, and under the doors
>Blood came hurrying from the work of the lion.
>The high priest of death, at the altar of corpses.

Excerpt 6
(*Cassandra calls upon Apollo to protect her.*)

>Apollo!
>No!
>O Earth! Earth!
>No! No!
>[. . .]
>Apollo! Earth! Oh
>No. No. No. Apollo!
>[. . .]
>Apollo! God of my guidance –
>You led me the whole long way
>Only to destroy me.

[. . .]
Apollo! God of my guidance –
What dreadful place have you brought me to?
[. . .]
A house that hates God.
A house that God hates.
Walls weeping blood
Housing butchered innocents,
The blood and the bones of children.
[. . .]
Running in blood. Look –
Look – the witnesses:
Children covering their eyes,
Sobbing blood through their fingers,
Children chopped up, screaming
And roasted and eaten
By their own father.
[. . .]
Look there. Now. A heart pounding
Thick with hatred
Behind the door. Evil
Is pouring out evil. Blood
Pours out of a body
That expected love.
Taken by surprise,
Naked, helpless –
Bound in the net of pitiless Fate
And coming through the meshes, the blade
Again and again.
[. . .]
She is washing her husband
In his own blood.
He reaches from the bath for her hand
As it jerks him into pitch darkness.
[. . .]
Now the net – the fish-eye terror:
Death is bundling him up, like a mother
Swaddling a child.
The woman who shared his bed

Is driving the bronze through him.
The Furies crowd into the house
Gorged with the blood of this house,
Ravenous for the blood of this house –
Look at the Furies. Look – look –
[. . .]
Oh!
The cow has gored the great bull.
And it's too late.
He thought it was his robe, it's the mesh of his death.
And the long horn's gone in.
And again. And again. He's wallowing
In a bath full of his own blood.
[. . .]
And I am there with him.
Look at me – like a dolphin split open
From end to end.
I roll in his blood.
Carved by the same blade.
Apollo–
Why have you tangled me in this man's
Horrible death?
[. . .]
The bird can fly
But I have to go down
Under the hammer-blow
That will empty me –
Like a chicken on a block.
[. . .]
Paris with his great love
Annihilated
His own family and his own city.
I grew by Scamander, happy.
That sweet stream.
But now the rivers of the land of the dead
Will flow with my prophecies.
[. . .]
Nothing could block the flight of my prophecy.
Troy's walls were not enough.

Her towers not enough.
The beasts slaughtered daily on every altar
Not enough.
Prayers, shields and the strong warriors behind them –
None of them were enough
To deflect my prophecy.
Nobody believed me.
Now they are all dead
And soon I shall be with them.
[. . .]
This house is full of demons.
The loathsome retinue
Of the royal blood.
Under these painted ceilings they flitter and jabber.
They huddle on every stair.
They laugh and rustle and whisper
Inside the walls.
They shift things, in darkness
They squabble and scream in cellars.
And they sing madness
Into the royal ears. Madness.
Till royal brother defiles the bed of his brother.
Did that happen?
The foundations of the house of Atreus
Split open when it happened,
And the evil poured out, up and out.
Isn't that true? Swear it's true.

Excerpt 7
(*Cassandra predicts her own horrible end.*)

Apollo! I can feel
The shock waves of my own death
Coming towards me.
Apollo, snatch me away somehow.
This lion-woman who coupled with a wolf
In her lord's absence –
She will kill me. She has whetted the bronze.

Like a witch mashing her herbs,
She swears to make her husband's brain whirl,
Pouring my blood into his,
Stirring our blood together in the same vat –
Corpses together since we arrived together.

Federico García Lorca

Born into a prosperous farming family near Granada, Federico García Lorca (1898–1936) was deeply influenced by the people and customs of the Andalusian countryside. As well as being a much translated poet and dramatist, Lorca was a talented musician. In Madrid, he was friendly with a number of the leading avant-garde artists, including the young Salvador Dalí. Celebrated for his poetry and lectures, he also became the foremost Spanish dramatist of his time. In 1929, after the success of *Romancero gitano*, he went to New York, returning to Spain at the optimistic outset of republican government; he was appointed director of La Barraca, a government-sponsored theatrical company, and it was during this time that he wrote and staged *Blood Wedding*. In 1936, the Civil War began. Lorca, suspected of republican sympathies, was arrested by Nationalist partisans and executed by firing squad.

Hughes's notebooks contain versions of several poems by Lorca. He refers also, in his essay on the artist Leonard Baskin, to Lorca's lecture 'Juego y teoría de duende' ('Play and Theory of the Duende'); see *Deep Song and Other Prose* of Federico García Lorca, edited and translated by Chrisopher Maurer, 1982). Lorca, in a way like D. H. Lawrence, distrusted print, or 'finished' writing, and his lectures, where he was stimulated by live audiences, contain some of his most resonant utterances; it is not hard to see why the theatre, especially folk theatre, should have appealed to him.

In particular, in his lecture on *duende*, Lorca confronts the perennial contradiction between a longing for form and order and a respect for chaos, the stifling of which may also stifle creativity. The term *duende* (elf, fairy, ghost, goblin, mischievous household spirit, from *dueño*, owner, lord of the house) is, according to Maurer, applied in Andalusia to the charm of certain gifted people, especially flamenco singers – 'The Andalusians say that a *cantaor* has *duende*.' For Lorca it was 'a protean earth spirit with three important traits: irrationality, demonism, and fascination with death'. Lorca describes how, '[a] few years ago, in a dancing contest at Jerez de la Frontera, an old woman of eighty carried off the prize against beautiful women and girls with waists like water, merely by raising her arms, throwing back her head, and stamping her foot on the platform; in that gathering of muses and angels, beauties of shape and beauties of smile, the moribund *duende*, dragging her wings of rusty knives along the ground, was bound to win and did in fact win.' However, he was also aware that if it be 'true that I am a poet by the grace of God – or the devil – I am also a poet by virtue of technique and effort, and knowing exactly what a poem is'.

Hughes discusses the healing powers of the imagination in his essay on the artist Leonard Baskin, 'The Hanged Man and the Dragonfly' (see Keith Sagar, *The Laughter of Foxes*, 2000, for detailed commentary): 'Lorca gave it a name, calling it the *duende* [. . .]. In his Arab/Andalusian setting he shows how naturally it can be taken for God – a divine horror – a thunderbolt beautiful and terrible [. . .]. [I]t seems to come from 'beyond death'. [. . .] Yet it is the core of life, like the black, ultimate resource of the organism. [. . .] The magical quality of a poem consists in its being always possessed by the *duende*, so that whoever beholds it is baptised with dark water. Because with *duende* it is easier to love and to understand; and this struggle for expression and for the communication of expression reaches at times, in poetry, the character of a fight to the death.' Lorca calls the creative energy *duende*; for Hughes it is *mana* – 'as the goddess of the source of terrible life, the real substance of any art that has substance, in spite of what we might prefer'. (See also 'Talking Without Words', in *Winter Pollen*, on Hughes's experience in Persia with *Orghast*.)

Leonard M. Scijaj (*Ted Hughes: Form and Imagination*, 1986) refers to Hughes's poem 'After Lorca': 'Though he certainly read Lorca and Kafka during this period, folklore and related primitive methods of solving "practical difficulties" provide the major sources for Hughes's surrealism in the sixties. Three influences converge here: his reviews of primitive folklore in the early sixties; his development of the concept of the poet as shaman, after a 1964 review of Eliade's *Shamanism*; and his (unpublished Bardo) libretto.' Ann Skea (*Ted Hughes: The Poetic Quest*, 1994) writes: 'Hughes's view of this universal spirit energy is not simple. He has spoken of it as Nature, the Goddess, Pan, and as an elemental demonic force. Like Lorca's *duende*, it is "the mystery, the roots fastened in the mire that we all know and all ignore, the mire that gives us the very substance of art". And like Lorca, and also Nietzsche, Hughes sees the necessity of confronting this demonic, magical power which exists around and within us, and also the danger of suppressing it, since it is an essential part of our whole being.'

The selection of poems by Lorca, translated by Hughes, is taken from the notebooks, in Emory University Library. The excerpts from *Blood Wedding* come from the translation published by Faber in 1996. The plot of *Blood Wedding* is based on an actual murder. It is one of a trilogy of rural tragedies, one of these, *Yerma*, having been translated by W. S. Merwin, whose translations – especially his version of medieval Spanish ballads – Hughes greatly admired. *Blood Wedding* had also been translated by the American writer Langston Hughes, in 1938. Hughes's version was produced at the Young Vic,

directed by Tim Supple, in September 1996. Hughes had also worked with
Supple on his translation of *Spring Awakening*, by Frank Wedekind, in 1995.

The Old Lizard [*El Lagarto Viejo*]

In the dried out path
I have seen the good lizard
(Drop of a crocodile)
In contemplation
In his green marriage coat
As of a devil's abbot
His tasteful bearing –
The stiff correct collar,
He has the mournful air
Of an ancient professor.
Those burned-out eyes
Of a broken artist –
How dismayed are they
Watching the afternoon.

Is this yours,
Friend is this
Your stroll at twilight.
Then you came for you are
Very old Mr Lizard,
And the children of the village
May well give you a scare.
What do you seek along the path,
Myopic thinker,
If the uncertain shortness
Of the parched afternoon
Has crumbled the horizon.

Do you want the blue charities
Of the dying heaven?
A halfpenny from a star?
Or perhaps
You have been reading a book
Of Lamartine, and you savour

The whorled silver trills
Of the birds.

(You watch the sun setting)
And your eyes reflect
Oh dragon of the frogs!
With a human light.
The oarless gondolas
Of thinking, traverse
The dark waters
Of your burned-out eyes.

Have you come searching
The beautiful she-lizard
Green as the wheatfields
In May are,
As long tresses
Oh sleeping pools
Who disdained you and after
Left you to your field?
O sweet idyll broken
Among the fresh reeds!
But live! The devil!
You have my sympathy.
The motto: 'I tread
On the "serpent" triumphs
And the great chin folds
Of a christian archbishop.'

Now the sun has dissolved.
In the cup of the mountains
And the dust of the flocks
Powders the roadways.
It is time to go:
Leave the scorched path,
Cease your meditation
You will have plenty of time
To admire the stars
When the worms
Eat you at their leisure.

Off to your home
Under the village of crickets.
Good night, my friend
Mr Lizard

Now there is no one in the field,
The mountains are dimmed
The road is empty.
Only from time to time
A cuckoo chimes in the darkness
Of the poplars.

Ballad of the Water of the Sea [*La Balada del Agua del Mar*]

The sea
Smiles far off.
Teeth of spume,
Lips of sky.

What do you sell, you wild girl
Of etc your breasts bare?

[Illegible: photocopy defective]
Of the sea.

What do you carry, you dark young man,
Mixed with your blood?

I carry, sir, the water
Of the sea.

Those salt tears,
Where do they come from, mother?

I weep, sir, the water
Of the sea!

Heart this bitter
Weight, where was it born?

Bitter, bitter is the water
Of the seas.

The sea
smiles far off.
Teeth of spume,
Lips of sky.

The Interrupted Concert [*El Concierto Interrumpido*]

The frozen drowsy pause
Of the half moon
Has broken the harmony
Of the deep night

The ditches protest silently,
Shrouded in hedges, [sedges?]
And the frogs, preachers of shadow,
Are mute.

In the old inn of the village
The sad music is over
And the most ancient star
Has doused [?] its look.

The wind has lain down in the caverns
Of the dark mountain
And a single poplar – the Pythagoras
Of the blank [?] plain –
Lifts its hundred year old hand
And strikes the moon.

Poem of the Saeta [*Poema de la Saeta*]

The dark archers
Come nearer Seville
     The open handed river.
Broad slow clouds
     My Guadalquivir.
They come from the remote
Regions of pain
     The open Guadalquivir

And they go to a labyrinth
Love, crystal & rock
    Ay, Guadalquivir.

Blood Wedding: Excerpt 1

(Act One, Scene 2: Leonardo's house. A song about a horse, a lullaby, which returns at the end of this ominous scene.)

MOTHER-IN-LAW
  Hush, baby, hush.
  Sing of the great horse
  That wouldn't drink the water.
  The water ran black
  Under the boughs.
  Under the bridge
  It stopped and sang.
  Who knows, my darling,
  The pain of the water
  That draws its long tail
  Through long green rooms.

WIFE
  Sleep, my blossom,
  The horse will not drink.

MOTHER-IN-LAW
  Sleep, little rose,
  The horse is weeping,
  Its hooves are hurt,
  Its mane is frozen.
  And in its eye
  A dagger of silver.
  Down by the river,
  Down by the river,
  Blood is pouring
  Stronger than the water.

WIFE
  Sleep, my blossom,
  The horse will not drink.

MOTHER-IN-LAW

    Sleep, little rose,
    The horse is weeping.

WIFE

    He will not touch
    The edge of the river
    He will not, he will not
    Quench his muzzle
    In the fringe of the river
    Though it sweats
    Flies of silver.
    He can only whinny
    To the hard mountains
    From the dry river
    Dead in his throat.
    Aye, the great horse
    That will not drink the water.
    The sorrow of the snows,
    The horse of dawn.

MOTHER-IN-LAW

    Keep away, stay
    Close to the window
    With a branch of dreams
    And a dream of branches.

WIFE

    Now my baby sleeps.

MOTHER-IN-LAW

    Now my baby rests.

WIFE

    Horse, my baby
    Has a soft pillow.

MOTHER-IN-LAW

    A cot of iron.

WIFE

    A cover of linen.

MOTHER-IN-LAW
Hush, baby, hush.

WIFE
Aye, the great horse
Will not drink the water.

MOTHER-IN-LAW
Keep away, stay,
Run to the mountain
And the dark valley
Of the mare.

WIFE
Now my baby sleeps.

MOTHER-IN-LAW
Now he can rest.

WIFE
Sleep, my blossom,
The horse will not drink.

MOTHER-IN-LAW
Sleep, little rose,
The horse is weeping.

Blood Wedding: Excerpt 2
(*Act Two, Scene 1: mother and son meeting with daughter and daughter's father and their servant.*)

SERVANT
Let the bride awake
On the morning of her wedding.
Let all the rivers of the world
Bear her flowering wreath.

BRIDE: (*smiling*)
Let's go.

SERVANT: (*dancing around her*)
　　Let her awaken
　　With the green branch
　　Of the flowering laurel.
　　Let her awaken
　　With the trunk and the branch
　　Of the laurel flowers.

　　[. . .]

VOICES
　　Let the bride awake
　　On the morning of her wedding.

BRIDE
　　Let the bride awake.

She runs out.

SERVANT
　　Here are the guests. (*To Leonardo*) Don't come near her again.

LEONARDO
　　You needn't worry.

He goes. It starts to get light.

FIRST GIRL
　　Let the bride awake
　　On the morning of her wedding.
　　Start dancing in a ring,
　　Hang flower wreaths
　　From every window.

VOICES
　　Let the bride awake.

SERVANT
　　Let her wake up
　　With the green branch
　　Of flowering laurel.
　　Let her wake up
　　With the trunk and the branch
　　Of the laurel flowers.

SECOND GIRL
    Let her awaken,
    Her long hair loose,
    Her bodice of snow.
    And over her brow,
    Flowers of jasmine.

SERVANT
    Ay, farmer's daughter,
    See the moon climb.

FIRST GIRL
    Ay, young man,
    Leave your broad hat
    On the bough of the olive.

FIRST YOUTH
    Let the bride awaken.
    The wedding guests are coming
    Across the far fields
    With baskets of dahlias,
    With loaves that are blest.

VOICES
    Let the bride awaken.

SECOND GIRL
    The bride, the bride
    Puts on her white wreath.
    The groom, the groom
    Ties it with gold ribbons.

SERVANT
    By the grapefruit tree
    The bride will lie awake.

THIRD GIRL
    By the orange tree
    The groom will give her
    Spoon and napkin.

    Three Guests enter.

FIRST GIRL
  O dove, awake,
  The dawn is brightening
  The bells of darkness.

GUEST
  The bride, the white bride,
  Today she's a maiden,
  Tomorrow a woman.

FIRST GIRL
  Come down, dark one,
  Dragging your train of silk.

GUEST
  Come down, little dark one,
  The morning dew is icy.

FIRST YOUTH
  Awake, bride, awake.
  Let the air carry
  The orange blossom.

SERVANT
  I shall embroider a tree
  Flowing with dark red ribbons,
  With long life, with children.

VOICES
  Let the bride awaken.

FIRST YOUTH
  On the morning of her wedding.

GUEST
  On the morning of your wedding
  How beautiful you are.
  Wife worthy a warrior,
  Flower of the mountain.

FATHER
  Wife worthy a warrior,
  The groom carries her off.

He is coming with oxen
To claim his prize.

THIRD GIRL
The groom is a golden flower.
Where his foot falls
Carnations spring up.

SERVANT
Oh my lucky child!

SECOND YOUTH
Let the bride awaken.

SERVANT
A beautiful bride!

FIRST GIRL
From every window
The wedding is calling.

SECOND GIRL
Let the bride come out.

FIRST GIRL
She's coming, she's coming!

SERVANT
Ring and ring again
Bells for the wedding.

FIRST GIRL
She's coming! She's here.

SERVANT
Now the wedding
Starts to move
Like a huge bull.

Bride appears. Guitars. Girls kiss the Bride.

Blood Wedding: Excerpt 3

(*Act Three, Scene 1: Three Woodcutters address the Moon. The
Moon sings. This passage ends with a Beggar Woman predicting
murder.*)

Brilliant light grows from left.

FIRST
The moon rises.
A moon with great leaves.

SECOND
Fill the blood with jasmine.

FIRST
Lonely moon.
Moon with great leaves.

SECOND
A wash of silver
On the face of the bride.

THIRD
Evil moon
Cover their love
With a shadowy branch.

FIRST
Sorrowful moon,
Cover their love
With a branch of shadow.

*Exit Woodcutters. Enter the Moon – a young woodcutter
with a white face. Intense blue light.*

MOON
Round swan on the river,
Round swan on the river,
Cathedral's eye.
And among the leaves
A false dawn –
I am all these things.
They cannot escape.

Who hides? Who weeps
In the shrubs of the valley?
The moon leaves a knife
Hanging in the sky –
An ambush of lead
That lies in wait
For the agony of blood.
Let me in! I'm freezing
On walls and windows.
Open your houses,
Open your hearts,
Let me in! Warm me.
I'm cold. My ashes
Of sleepy metal climb
To the crests of fire
On roofs, on mountains.
Snow carries me
On shoulders of jasper.
And water drowns me
Cold and hard,
In every pool.
Tonight there'll be blood
To warm my cheeks.
Let there be no shadow,
No secret corner
To keep them safe.
I want to slide
Into a bosom
Where I can be warm.
A heart for me!
Warm, spilling warm
Over the mountains
Of my breast
Let me in. Let me in.

To the branches.

I don't want shadows.
I want my beams
To pierce every cranny.

Among dark trees,
A rumour of glitters.
Tonight there'll be blood
To warm my cheeks.
Who hides? Come out.
They won't escape.
I'll make the horse flash
With a fever of diamonds.

Moon disappears among tree-trunks. Darkness. Old Beggar
Woman appears in her dark green cloth. Feet bare. Face hardly seen
among the folds.

BEGGAR WOMAN
The moon goes in and they come nearer.
Here they shall stay. The lacerated
Flight of their screams
Will be stifled
By the voice of the trees, and the voice of the river.
This is the place. This is the time.
I am tired. On bedroom floors
The coffins lie open.
The white sheets are spread
For heavy bodies
With their throats cut. And the birds
Will go on sleeping. The wind
Will bundle their cries
In her skirt and fly off with them
Over the dark trees,
Or bury them
In soft mud.
The moon! The moon!

Moon appears, with the blue light.

Blood Wedding: Excerpt 4

(*Act Three, Scene 1: The Bride and Leonardo; Beggar Woman describes the deaths of the Bridegroom and Leonardo; the Bride speaks of her passion for Leonardo; the mother laments.*)

BRIDE
I will sleep at your feet,
I will guard your dreams,
Naked, looking out at the fields,
Like a hound bitch.
That's what I am!
I look at you
And your beauty burns me.

LEONARDO
Flame makes flame.
One small flame
Can destroy
Two grains of corn
Lying together.
We must go.

[. . .]

BEGGAR WOMAN
I saw them. They'll soon be here. Two torrents lying without
a movement, among the great stones. Two men at the feet
of a horse. Dead in the beauty of the night. Dead, yes, dead.

FIRST GIRL
Oh, I can't bear to hear it.

BEGGAR WOMAN
Their eyes broken flowers.
Their teeth two fistfuls
Of frozen snow.
They fell together
And the bride returns
With their blood in her hair,
And on her skirt.
They're coming now,
Covered by blankets,

Carried by tall young men.
It happened. And that's it.
And it was right.
Over the golden flower, dirty sand.

She goes. Girls begin to go.

FIRST GIRL
Dirty sand.

SECOND GIRL
On the golden flower.

LITTLE GIRL
On the golden flower.
They're bringing, the dead from the river,
One dark-skinned,
The other, dark-skinned.
Over the golden flower
The shadow of a nightingale
Flutters and sobs.

All go. Mother and Neighbour enter. Neighbour sobbing.

MOTHER
Be quiet.

NEIGHBOUR
I can't help it.

MOTHER
I said be quiet. (*At the door*) Is anybody there? (*Puts her
hands to her forehead.*) My son should have answered.
But my son's nothing now – an armful of dry flowers. A
faint voice the other side of the mountains. (*Angrily to
Neighbour*) Will you be quiet. I want no weeping in this
house. Your tears are just tears, they come from your eyes.
My tears are different. When I'm alone my tears will come
from the soles of my feet. From my very roots. And they'll
burn hotter than blood.

NEIGHBOUR
Come with me to my house. You can't stay here.

MOTHER

I want to be here. Here. Peaceful. Now they're all dead.
At midnight I'll sleep. And I shan't be afraid of a gun or a
knife. Other mothers will go to their windows, lashed by the
rain, looking for the face of their sons. Not me. And out of
my sleep I'll make a cold marble dove to carry camellias of
frost to the graveyard. No, not to the graveyard. It's not a
graveyard. It's a bed of earth, a cradle that shelters them and
rocks them in the sky.

[. . .]

BRIDE

Because I went off with the other one. Yes, I went. You
would have done the same. I was a woman on fire. Inside
and outside ablaze with agonies. Your son was a single drop
of water that I hoped would give me children, and health:
the other was a dark big river, carrying torn-up trees, that
brought me the sounds of its reeds and its song. And I was
going with your son, your little boy of cold water. But the
other sent thousands of birds that stopped me and dropped
frost into the wounds of this poor, shrivelling woman, this
girl possessed by flames. I didn't want to! Do you hear me? I
didn't want to. My whole hope was your son and I haven't
deceived him. But the other's arm dragged me like a wave
from the sea. And it would always have dragged me, always,
even if I'd been an old woman and all your son's sons had
tried to hold me down by my hair.

[. . .]

MOTHER

Neighbours. With a knife,
With a small knife,
On an appointed day
Between two and three in the morning,
Two men who were in love
Killed each other.
With a knife,
With a small knife
That hardly fits the hand
But slides in clean

Through surprised flesh
Till it stops
There,
In the quivering
Dark
Roots
Of the scream.

Here is a knife,
A small knife
That barely fits the hand,
Fish without scales or river,
On an appointed day
Between two and three in the morning
This knife
Left two men stiffening
With yellow lips.
It barely fits the hand
But slides in cold
Through startled flesh
Till it stops, there,
In the quivering
Dark
Roots
Of the scream.

Anonymous (The *Pearl* Poet)

Nothing is known of the author of *Sir Gawain and the Green Knight*, which is roughly contemporary with Chaucer's *The Canterbury Tales* in the latter part of the fourteenth century. It is written in a dialect belonging to Cheshire, Lancashire or Staffordshire, more remote to modern readers than Chaucer's language, based in London. It survives in a single manuscript copy of about 1400, along with three other poems (*Pearl, Patience* and *Cleanness*) probably by the same writer. The poem is written in alliterative metre, derived from a tradition predating the Norman Conquest, different from that associated with Chaucer, which reflected contemporary Italian and French models, although the verse form used by the Gawain poet and others was somewhat less rigorous than the tight alliterative metre of Anglo-Saxon epic poetry. The alliterative long line is noticeably more flexible than the classic iambic pentameter line of English verse from Spenser on. As Brian Stone characterises it (in *Sir Gawain and the Green Knight*, Penguin, 2nd edition, 1974):

> Together with their chosen form, the alliterative poets kept the distinctive qualities of the northern epos; the stark realism of Norse and Anglo-Saxon literature, the harsh natural setting, its frequent combination of violent event, laconic understatement and grim humour, its continuous strength and moral seriousness. [. . .] [I]n subject matter and tone they showed themselves capable of absorbing the entire Romance scheme of things, including the whole apparatus of chivalric courts and courtly love. The fusion of these elements gives *Sir Gawain and the Green Knight* its extraordinary richness. [. . .] Its outlandish quality derives partly from its language which contains many hard-sounding words of Norse origin which are rare or non-existent in Chaucer, and partly from its expression of an early medieval northern culture which was to be largely submerged in a rival culture, the one based on the London-Oxford-Cambridge triangle and destined to become ours.

In a long essay, 'Myth, Metre, Rhythms' (1993; included in *Winter Pollen*), Hughes contrasts the early prosody, based on accent and speech rhythms, as exemplified in *Gawain*, with what he calls the 'new orthodoxy', resulting from metrical reforms, and typical of Surrey's verse (as against Wyatt's), based on French and Italian models (e.g., Petrarch), prosodic reforms which had begun with Chaucer. He traces a genealogy, the history of these changes, in which he clearly perceives a loss, or at least a distancing from the language as spoken:

> In retrospect one can see that his publication [Tottel's *Miscellany* of 1557] announced the final triumph of a process that had visibly begun with Chaucer, who first introduced those continental models of metre and versification. [. . .] [N]ow, quite suddenly [. . .], the powers of the new orthodoxy had become absolute. Tottel's ideal was Petrarch. His verse specimens, in the *Miscellany*, were meant to provide models of metrically correct prosody for the courtly versifiers of the new high culture, and a standard for 'the stateliness of the stile removed from the rude skill of common ears'. Even more ominously, according to this new orthodoxy Wyatt and the old poetry were hopelessly crippled by 'the bondage of speech', while correct metres were gracefully free of any such base limitation. Already, that is, the strictly metrical tradition's hostility to the 'rhythms of common speech' had asserted itself, as a law of the land.

According to Hughes, Wyatt's music became more audible to readers when that of G. M. Hopkins did, the process owing much to Eliot and Pound, 'ears from right outside the historically closed cognitive system of the English orthodoxy'. Hughes takes *Sir Gawain and the Green Knight* as an exemplar of the old system, very hard to come to terms with for modern readers:

> The problem that Wyatt's apparently crippled lines presented to Tottel [. . .] is closely paralleled by the problem that the alliterative lines of *Gawain and the Green Knight* have represented to scholars up to this moment. Wyatt, like Chaucer, was clearly able to hear – and appreciate – the music of the *Gawain* line or of the verse in that tradition. Both could still use what they wanted of it – Wyatt wanting a little more than Chaucer.
>
> In fact, Wyatt's hand-wrought, gnarled, burr-oak texture owes more than a little to the alliterative tradition. [. . .] It was there – somewhere between Wyatt and Tottel (only a generation) – that all understanding of that alliterative tradition, as an evolved and sophisticated form of verbal music, seems to have been finally lost. At least, as far as the high culture and the new orthodoxy were concerned, it was lost. [. . .]
>
> When native poets jibbed at the constraints, and felt the need to search experimentally for a more varied music, they tended to search higher in the high culture, and tinkered with classical metres, as did Sidney and his circle, and Campion. In all that time, it seems, nobody made any attempt to introduce or adapt or make anything new of the old metre of the *Gawain* tradition. As if every memory trace of it had gone.

Hughes evidently intended to translate the whole poem, but published only one section, in the anthology *The School Bag* (edited by Seamus Heaney and Ted Hughes, Faber, 1997). His notebooks, however, contain a draft of substantially more than this, from the beginning of the poem. Apart from wishing to acquaint himself more closely with *Gawain* and to extract a narrative which would convey to modern readers something of its combination of fierceness and good (or black) humour, one may surmise that he was also experimenting with the possibility of reactivating a tradition of orally based poetry that he saw as having been broken. He is particularly alive to the comedy, the aura of salubriousness of the poem. He does not focus upon exact reproduction of the alliteration, although alliteration is certainly a feature of his translation, as too is the long, four-stress, non-iambic line. At the same time, he borrows freely from contemporary and non-contemporary usage. His version of *Gawain* is visually focused and might even seem to lend itself to a filmic or theatrical treatment, as did his translation of the *Metamorphoses*. In a word, Hughes, like Chapman or Golding before him, seems intent on telling or retelling the story vividly for a contemporary audience, adhering, to the extent that this is compatible with these aims, to the rhythms and texture of the source. In this case, the compatibility was pronounced, since contemporary West Yorkshire diction echoes the earlier form of the language.

It cannot be stressed enough, I think, that Hughes was particularly sensitive to the requirements of absorbing narration (see, for instance, his 1965 review of the writings of the Yiddish writer Isaac Bashevis Singer, 'Revelations: The Genius of Isaac Bashevis Singer', reprinted in *Winter Pollen*; Singer's stories, he felt, held the attention, there being nothing superfluous or redundant, nothing to impede the flow). Hughes was not writing for scholars, or even for the scholarly, so much as for 'ordinary readers' – also, of course, for himself, wanting to narrow the gap between teller and told, even over such a distance in time. His text, thus, demands to be read through from start to finish, without interruption. To the present writer, this seems to have more to do with focus or concentration than with facileness or avoidance of technical difficulties. It is 'the heart's tone' (Pound's term) that Hughes, who found the Gawain poem close to his own heart, sought to preserve. He aims, apparently, at a combination of formality and naturalness. What Pound said of Arthur Golding, the Tudor translator of Ovid's *Metamorphoses*, that '[h]e is intent on conveying a meaning, and not on bemusing them with a rumble', might well be applied to Hughes as well.

Excerpts from Parts I and II of the poem are taken from Hughes's manuscripts, followed by a portion of Part IV, which was first published in *The School Bag*. Thanks are due to Keith Sagar for help in transcribing the manuscript material.

The setting is King Arthur's court, in the midst of festivities, lasting from Christmas to New Year. Suddenly the Green Knight, a gigantic figure, appears. He issues a challenge to the King or any of his knights, to strike him with his axe, but in return to seek him out in the Green Chapel, a year from then, to receive a blow in return. Gawain accepts the challenge on the King's behalf.

From Part I

He must have been the tallest man on the earth
Between the neck and the navel so broad and so deep
And his loins and limbs so long and so heavy.
As earth's men go, I think he was near-giant
Far the biggest anyway, among men
And yet, for such a bulk, on a horse the most graceful.
Though his chest and shoulder were colossal
Belly and waist were wonderfully slender,
His every feature cut to the same fashion
    So clean.
  But what amazed them all
  Was his colour.
  He came on dangerously,
  Crown to toe dense green.

The man's face and flesh were as green as his garments.
The long jacket that fitted close to his figure,
Over it all a full cloak, lined [?]
With a wealth of [?] fur, its edging dazzle
A blaze of pure ermine the same as the hood
That fell back over his long hair and his shoulders.
Leggings tight and neat of the one green
Clung to his calves, the spurs glistening below them,
Gold, and richly patterned their silk fittings –
But his feet [?] bare, for he rode shoeless,
The man's entire garb green as grass,
The buckles of his belt and the bright stones
That studded his superb array so [?],
Set in silk, all over himself and his saddle.
Nobody could number half the details
Worked into what he wore, the birds and the flies
Brilliant green under green, the gold thread within it.
The pendants of his harness, the hind crupper,
The bosses of the bit, the stirrups he stood in,
Every glitter of metal enamelled the same,
His saddlebows the same, and their deep skirts
That busily flashed and glowed with their green jewels.

And the great horse he rode on all the one colour
    The same
  A massively-built green horse
  A big beast hard to manage,
  Restive on a tight rein –
  Very like his master.

This fellow in full green was strangely merry,
The hair of his head resembled his horse's
A mane straight and thick draped his shoulders
While a thick bush of beard hung over his breast,
Both cropped to a length just short of his elbows
So half his arms were hidden by his own hair
Like the hood and shoulder-cape of a King
And the mane of his horse was much like this,
Combed and handsomely curled, with many a knot
Gold thread braided in with the sheer green
Beside each twist of hair a twist of gold
The forelock and the tail dressed like each other
Both crossbound with a gleam of green ribbon
Set with costly stones to the tip of the tresses
And tight-laced at the crest with an intricate knot
Where bells clustered and jingled their burnished gold.
Such a horse on this earth and hero to ride him
Nobody in that hall had ever set eyes on
    Before.
  His lance was like lightning –
  So said all that saw him.
  It seemed no man could survive
  A blow from him.

Yet he carried neither helmet nor hauberk,
No neck-armour, no plate fettled for combat,
No shield and no spear to prick or to pierce
But in one hand he held a bunch of holly
That glows its brightest green when groves are barest
And in the other an axe, enormous and ugly,
A pitiless weapon for any to touch in verse.
And a full stride long was the massive head,
The spike of green steel inlaid with gold

The blade polished bright, with broad edge,
Set as keen to shear as the daintiest razor.
The helve he gripped it by was a thick stave
Bound with iron the entire length to the heel
Fantastically wrought with green engraving
A lanyard slung from it, lashed at the head
Then looped round and round the length of the shaft
End to end hung with rich tassels attached
To big knots of the green elaborately braided.
This was the apparition that entered the hall
Rode straight to the high dais, afraid of nothing
Greeting nobody, looking over all heads.
The first word he uttered: 'Where', he cried,
'Is the head of this assembly? That is the man
I shall be pleased to meet and to speak with
　　A word for a word.'
　He rode up and down,
　Looking in all the faces.
　He stopped and he studied
　He found the most famous.

[. . .]

Then Arthur rises to face the uncanny stranger,
Greets him with courtesy, fearless as ever
Saying 'We welcome you, under this roof.
I am head of all here. My name is Arthur.
Dismount and join us awhile I beg you.
Whatever your errand may be, tell us later.'
'No' replied the Knight, 'by High-Heaven,
To linger here was no part of my purpose.
But because your name, Lord, is so famous
Your city and your host known for the best,
The hardest of all on horseback in their armour
The bravest and the noblest men on earth
Well-tested players in other noble pastimes,
And because courtesy, it is told, will be found here,
This has brought me to you, on this day.
You can be sure, by the green branch I bear
I come not an enemy but in peace.

Had I been looking for battle, dressed for battle,
I have at home both hauberk and helmet
Both shield and sharp spear brightly polished
And other hardy weapons, I can tell you,
But since I want no strife, dressed for ease.
Now if you are as brave as you are boasted
You will happily meet me in the arms
      I ask for.'
   Arthur replied: 'Courteous
   As you are, if you offer
   To fight without armour
   You will not lack takers.'

'No, truly I am not here looking for conflict.
I see none on these benches but beardless infants.
If I were on a big horse buckled in armour
None in this hall could match me, all are too feeble.
Therefore I have a Christmas game to play
For it is Yule and New Year, and here are warriors.
If any among you thinks he is man enough,
Blood bold enough, wits wild enough,
To dare to strike full strength, then stand for the same
I shall give him this great axe as a gift
This massive, marvellous weapon, to use as he pleases.
I'll undergo the first blow, bare as I am.
If any man has the heart to meet this challenge,
Here is the axe, let him leap up and take it,
I have no more claim on it, it is his own,
And I shall stand stock still to receive his stroke.
If you will grant me the right to give him the same
      In return,
   And yet I allow him respite
   A twelvemonth and a day.
   Now, quickly, who
   Dare say something to this?'

[. . .]

The King commanded Gawain to stand.
Instantly up, stepping forward lightly

He kneeled before the King, and took that weapon.
The King yielded it to him, and lifting a hand
Gave him God's blessing, and bade him
Keep his head and heart alike stalwart.
'Remember, nephew, a single blow,' said the King,
'Dealt as you should deal it, as I fancy
The return blow might not much hurt you.'
Gawain with the axe steps close to the Knight
Who waits for him there, quite unalarmed and at ease.
Then the Green Knight speaks to Sir Gawain:
'Let us rehearse the terms, before we go further.
First I must ask you, sir, what is your name?
Tell me this openly, that I may trust you.'
'In good faith', said the noble Knight, 'I am Gawain
Who gives you this blow, and, no matter what follows,
Will take from you, in a twelvemonth, the same blow
With any weapon you choose, but from you only
    Of all men.'
  The other spoke again:
  'Sir Gawain I swear
  I am very happy
  To take this stroke from you.'

'By God,' said the Green Knight, 'you have pleased me
That I shall get as your gift what I asked for here.
And point by point you have recounted rightly
The whole of my wager, as I put it to Arthur.
But now you must give me your word, sir, on your honour,
You will come seeking me out wherever you think
I might be found alive, to collect such payment
As this great court sees you hand me today.'
'Where shall I find you,' asked Gawain, 'where is your
    place?
By God who made me, how can I know where you live?
I never heard of you, of your court or your name.
Let me know then, truly, tell me your name,
And I shall do all I can to be there on the day.
I swear this as a vow, on my honour.
Enough there for the New Year. I need no more.'

Said the Man in Green to noble Gawain:
'If I utter the truth, when I have this word
And you have skilfully dealt it, I shall tell you clearly
My house, my home, my name enough
For you to test my word and keep your promise.
But [? line missing]
Then you can rest at home and look no further –
    But enough.
  Now take that pitiless weapon,
  Show how you strike.'
  'Gladly, so,' said Gawain,
  And he fingered the blade's edge.

Now the Green Knight made himself ready
Bowed his head a little, and baring the flesh,
Folded over his crown the long bright hair,
[? line missing]
Gawain gripped the axe and heaved it upward.
His left foot forward taking the full weight
He brought it down so hard on the bare skin
The shearing edge sundered the man's bone,
Sliced through all the muscle, and severed it.
The noble head leapt from its neck to the floor
And rolled under the benches, where feet spurned it.
Blood spouted from the body, shining on the green
Yet he neither fell nor even faltered.
Unshaken he strode forward on firm legs,
Shouldered the knights asunder, and reaching out
Grabbed his [?] head and hoisted it high
Then turned back to his horse, and caught at the bridle,
Stepped into the stirrup and vaulted astride.
All this time the head hanging from his hand
And settled himself into the saddle
As if he were unharmed, though he sat headless
    There.
  He twisted his body,
  That ghastly bloody trunk,
  And many were appalled
  Afresh as he spoke.

For he holds his head on high, in his hand
And turning the face towards those at the high table
As the eyelids lift and the great eyes stare,
As the mouth moves these words come from it:
'Gawain, see that you honour your word in full.
Search for me faithfully, so, till you find me,
As you have sworn and as all these knights have witnessed.
I charge you now to seek the Green Chapel,
And take back the blow you have dealt, as you have
    earned it,
On New Year's Morning render it promptly.
Many know me: the Knight of the Green Chapel,
So if you search to find me, you cannot fail.
Either come, or win the name of a coward.'
With a fierce wrench at the reins he spins his horse,
And [?] out through the hall door, his head in his hand,
The flint sparks flashing from under the horse's hooves.
Nobody knew to what land he had gone,
Any more than they knew where he had come from.
        What now?
    The King and Gawain laugh
    At the green marvel.
    Yet all had to agree
    It surely was a marvel.

From Part II

After the summer season, with her kind winds
When Zepherus breathes life into seeds and grasses
Delightful is the lush herbage that thickens
Under the quenching dews that drop from the leaves
To flash a rainbow blaze at the bright sun.
But harvest follows hard, urging the crop
Warning it to ripen before the frost falls.
Autumn's baking winds harry the dust
Off the earth and high up into the air.
Angry winds wrestle [?] with the sun.
Leaves fly from the boughs and are whisked over earth.

Grass that was all green is all grey.
Whatever sprung in spring rots or ripens –
The year is gone in a huddle of yesterdays
And winter has come wandering back, as it must
    In this world.
  Till the moon of Michaelmas
  Brings winter's first touch,
  And suddenly Gawain
  Is thinking of his promise.

And yet until All Hallows he lingers with Arthur
Who that day made a feast to honour Gawain
With rich celebrations at the Round Table,
The women beautiful and the knights gentle.
For love of that fine lord all felt anxious
But never let it lessen their merriment.
Many who grieved for Gawain let jests fly.
After the meal, he turned to his Uncle
[? line missing]
'Liege lord of my life, I must ask your leave.
You know what this matter amounts to, I do not want
To burden you with it, never more than a trifle.
But without fail I am bound for the blow, tomorrow,
To find this giant in green, as God will guide me.'
Then the pick of the court gathered together,
Owen and Eric, and a whole crowd of others,
Sir Dodinal le Sauvage, the duke of Clarence,
Lancelot and Lionel, and the good Lucan,
Sir Bois and Sir Bedivere, both big men,
Mador de la Port, and many more of the best.
This group of courtiers clustered about the King
All careful to give Gawain good counsel.
Much sorrow was stifled in that hall
[? line missing]
Seeing one true as Gawain [?] on that errand,
To collect a fatal blow, and never again
    Draw sword.
  But Gawain only laughed
  Saying: 'What is there to fear?

Whether it's harsh or gentle,
What can I do but test it?'

From Part IV

(*Gawain arrives at the Green Chapel to keep his word.*)

Then he spurred Gringolet, and took up the trail.
Trees overhung him, the steep slope close to his shoulder.
He pushed on down through the rough, to the gorge-bottom.
Wherever he turned his eyes, it looked wilder.
Nothing anywhere near that could be a shelter.
Only cliffy brinks, beetling above him.
Knuckled and broken outcrops, with horned crags.
Clouds dragging low, torn by the scouts.
There he reined in his horse and puzzled awhile,
Turning his doubts over, he searched for the Chapel.
Still he could see nothing. He thought it strange.
Only a little mound, a tump, in a clearing,
Between the slope and the edge of the river, a knoll.
Over the river's edge, at a crossing place,
The burn bubbling under as if it boiled.
The Knight urged his horse and came closer.
He dismounted there, light as a dancer,
And tethered his costly beast to a rough branch.
Then he turned to the tump. He walked all round it,
Debating in himself what it might be.
Shaggy and overgrown with clumps of grass,
It had a hole in the end, and on each side.
Hollow within, nothing but an old cave
Or old gappy rock-heap, it could be either
        Or neither.
    'Ah God!' sighed Gawain,
    'Is the Green Chapel here?
    Here, about midnight,
    Satan could say a prayer.'

'Surely,' he muttered, 'this is desolation.
This oratory is ugly, under its weeds.

The right crypt for that ogre, in his greenery,
To deal with his devotions devil-fashion.
My five wits warn me, this is the evil one,
Who bound me on oath to be here, to destroy me.
The chapel of Mischance – God see it demolished!
It is the worst-cursed Church I ever attended.'
With his helmet on his head, and his lance in his hand,
He clambered up on top of the bushy cell
And heard coming off the hill, from a face of rock,
The far side of the stream, a ferocious din.
What! It screeched in the crag, as if it would split it!
It sounded like a scythe a-shriek on a grind-stone!
What! It grumbled and scoured, like water in a mill!
What! It rushed and it rang, painful to hear!
'By God!' thought Gawain, 'I think that scummer
Is done in your honour, Knight, to welcome you
     As you deserve.
  Let God have his way! Ah well,
  It helps me not one bit.
  What if I lose my life?
  No noise is going to scare me.'

Then the Knight shouted, at the top of his voice:
'Is nobody at home, to collect my debt?
Gawain is here, now, walking about.
If any man is willing, get here quickly.
It is now or never, if he wants payment.'
'Be patient,' came a voice from the crag overhead,
'And I shall satisfy you, as I promised.'
Then he was back at his racket, with fresh fury,
Wanting to finish his whetting, before he came down.
But suddenly he was there, from under a cliff,
Bounding out of a den with a frightful weapon –
A Dane's axe, new fettled to settle the wager.
It had a massive head hooking back to the helve,
Ground bright with a file, and four foot long.
It measured as much by the rich thong that hung from it.
That giant, all got up in green as before,
Both the face and the legs, the hair and the beard,

Came down with plunging strides, in a big hurry,
Planting the axe to the earth and striding beside it.
When he got to the water he would not wade it,
He vaulted across on his axe, and loomed up,
Bursting into the clearing, where he stood
        On the snow.
    Sir Gawain knew how to greet him –
    But not too friendly.
    While the other replied: 'I see, Sir Sweetness,
    A man can keep his word.'

'Gawain,' said the Green Man. 'God protect you.
Let me welcome you, Knight, to my small holding.
You have timed your coming, as a true man should.
I see you honour the contract sealed between us.
This time twelvemonth back you took a thing from me.
So now, at this New Year, I shall reclaim it.
We have this lonely valley to ourselves.
No Knights are here to part us. We fight as we please.
Get that helmet off, and take your payment.
And give me no more talk than I gave you
When you whipped off my head with a single swipe.'
'Nay,' said Gawain. 'By God that gave me my soul,
I shall not grudge one jot of the damage coming.
Stick to the single stroke and I shall not move
Nor utter a word to warn you from whatever
        You choose.'
    He stretched his neck and bowed
    And bared the white flesh,
    Pretending to fear nothing.
    He would not dare to be fearful.

The Man in Green was eager, and all ready,
Grasping that ugly tool, to hit Gawain.
With all his body's might he hoisted it high,
Aimed it murderously for the utmost hurt.
And if he had brought it down as he had aimed it
The Knight who had never flinched would have been
        headless.
But Gawain skewed a sidelong glance at the weapon

[169]

As it came down to cut him off from the earth,
And shrank his shoulders a little from the sharp iron.
That other checked his stroke. He deflected the blade.
Then he reproached the prince with shaming words:
'You are not Gawain,' he said, 'whose name is so great,
Who never quailed in his life, by hill nor by vale.
Here you are wincing for fear before I touch you.
I never heard such cowardice of that hero,
When you hit me, I never fluttered an eyelid.
I never let out a squeak, in Arthur's hall.
My head rolled over the floor, but I did not flinch.
Before you are touched, your heart jumps out of your body.
It seems to me that I am a warrior far
    Far better.'
  Said Gawain: 'I winced once.
  And that once is the last.
  Though my head rolling on earth
  Can never be replaced.

'But hurry up, warrior, for God's sake come to the point.
Deal me my destiny, and do it quickly.
I shall stand to your stroke with not one stir
Till your axe-head hits me. I give you my word.'
'Then here it comes,' cried the other, and heaved it upwards
With a gargoyle grimace as if he were mad,
And with all his strength hauled down, yet never touched
  him.
He stopped the blade mid-stroke, before it could harm.
Gawain patiently waited, not a nerve twitched.
He stood there still as a rock or some stiff stump
That grips the stony ground with a hundred roots.
Then the Man in Green spoke pleasantly:
'Now that your heart is whole again, may I ask you,
Let your high rank, that Arthur gave you, preserve you
And recover your neck from my stroke, if it is able.'
Then Gawain ground his teeth and shouted in anger:
'Why, hack away, you savage, you threaten too long,
I think you have frightened yourself with your bragging.'
'What's this?' cried the other, 'Rough words from Sir Gawain?

I will no longer withhold from such an appeal
    Justice.'
  And he braced himself for the stroke –
  Clenching both lip and brow.
  No wonder he did not like it
  Who saw no rescue now.

Lightly he lifted the weapon, then let it down deftly
With the barb of the bit by the bare neck,
And though he swung full strength he hardly hurt him,
But snicked him on that side, so the sheer edge
Sliced through skin and fine white fat to the muscle,
Then over his shoulders the bright blood shot to the earth.
When Gawain saw his blood blink on the snow
He sprang a spear's length forward, in one great stride,
Snatched up his helmet as he went, and crammed it on his
    head.
A shunt of his shoulders brought his shield to the front
And his sword flashed out as he spoke fiercely:
Since he was first a man born of his mother
Never in this world was he half as happy.
'That's enough, warrior. I take no more.
I have taken the payment blow, without resistance.
If you fetch me another, I shall match it.
I shall repay it promptly, you can trust me,
    And in full.
  I owed a single cut.
  That was our covenant
  Agreed in Arthur's Hall –
  So now, Sir, what about it?'

The Knight in Green stepped back, and leaned on his axe.
Setting the shaft in the snow, he rested on the head
And gazed awhile at the prince who stood before him:
Armed, calm, fearless, undaunted. He had to admire him.
Now as he spoke, his voice was big and cheerful:
'What a brave fellow you are. Do not be angry.
Nobody here has misused you, or done you dishonour.
We kept to the terms agreed in the King's Court.
I promised a blow. You have it. You are well paid.

And I require from you no other quittance.
If I had wanted it, I could have grieved you.
I could have exacted a cut, perhaps, far worse.
But see how I teased you, my worst was a playful feint.
I did not maim you with a gash. I took only justice,
For the contract we agreed on that first night.
You have kept faith with me and the bond between us,
And all that you took you returned – as a good man
    should.'

Abdulah Sidran

Abdulah Sidran was born in 1944 in Bosnia and studied literature at Sarajevo University. Besides poetry, he has also written scripts and screen plays. He lives in Sarajevo.

The poems below all come from *Scar on the Stone: Contemporary Poetry from Bosnia*, edited by Chris Agee (Bloodaxe, 1998). Twenty-two poets are represented, translated by a number of English, American and Irish poets, including Ted Hughes (four in the collection). Most of the translations are based on literal versions by Antonela Glavinic. In his correspondence with the editor (see Appendix 14), Hughes expressed his preference for a kind of minimal translation; he is anxious, above all, not to mislead the reader by substituting his own interpretation. In his 'Notes for Translators' Chris Agee attached essays by János Csokits and Hughes, and Antonela Glavinic adopted a similar approach to that of Csokits, so that one supposes that Ted Hughes must have felt particularly comfortable with this assignment.

The translations below are by Ted Hughes and Antonela Glavinic. See Appendix 14 for Glavinic's version of the first two stanzas of 'Gavrilo'.

Gavrilo
[*Gavrilo Princip was the assassin of the Archduke Ferdinand in Sarajevo in 1914.*]

> The night is unreal, quiet, like hell –
> Which does not exist. The world,
> Its houses, its clutter, lies
> Deep in oil. This is the moment for you,
> The hesitant one, the undecided, to go
> Down that rotten stair, your hand
> Feeling for that wall, touching the oil,
> Saying: Come on, my heart, let's get the weapons! Because
>
> The night is so unreal –
> And far too quiet. And there is no one
> To tell us: Tomorrow, for you – horror.

Tomorrow, for you – love. The skull fills
With a terrible brightness. Hurry, hurry, the weapons –
Before the bone splits in the glare.
Somewhere close they are forging a shield – a true

And real shield, and this darkness
Embroiders for you, my heart, a warm cloak,
For you, everything, my shaking heart. We have to
Hurry, before the bone cracks, and dawn comes
Bursting our ear-drums with the screams from the street
And we suck in air mixed with hot shrapnel.
Hurry, hurry, my heart, get the weapons, before it dawns –

Before our god dies. Afterwards
There will be nobody to talk to
And nothing to talk with.
We'll be lying dead under the oil
In darkness – under the deaf
Heavy blunt years that press down
On this century's shoulders as this night
So unreal so overfull of brightness
Presses on my shoulders – crying Hurry
Hurry, my heart, let's get the weapons!

A Blind Man Sings to His City

The rain stops. Now from the drains,
From the attics, from under the floorboards
Of the shattered homes in the suburbs
Oozes the stench of the corpses
Of mice. I walk seeking
No special meaning in this. A blind man,
To whom it has been given to see
Only what others don't. This
Makes up for my deprivation: in the south wind
That touches me I recognise the voices
Of those who left this city. As if they were crying.
There, scent of the linden trees, close.
I know

The bridge is near, where my step and my stick
Will ring differently – more light
In the sound. There, now, right by my ear
Two flies mate in the air.
It will be scorching hot again. Bodies
Brush past me, hot,
Smelling of bed, smelling of lust. I walk muttering
To God, as if He were beside me:
'Surely nobody knows this city
Better than me – better than me, God,
To whom you have given never to see
The face he loves.'

Chronicle of a Miracle
'I have never seen anything for the first time.'

With your left hand
You push a thick mass of hair back from your forehead and
As your hand moves I have shifted
That gesture into memory and already
No longer see you push hair with hand from forehead
But am remembering how with your left hand
You push a thick mass of hair back from your forehead

You say with a voice that trembles
And stirs the candle-flame on the table in front of us
'It's stormy outside' and something not me but
Where there is some part of me (and what a part)
Shifts that voice into memory so that I am not
Only listening to you I am remembering
Listening to you and remembering your voice
That trembles and stirs the candle-flame on the table
In front of us and remembering
The evening and the voice saying 'It's stormy outside'

And it goes on being stormy outside and the evening
Goes on just as the life goes on which
No I don't seem to be living only remembering
Like the voice with which you are still saying

'It's stormy outside' the voice I remember like
The hand with which you push a mass of hair back from
   your forehead
As you speak the hand I remember, touching it
For the first time.

Jean Racine

Jean Racine (1639–99) was born into a religious family associated with Port Royal, centre of Jansenism, an evangelical Catholic sect, the poet himself being educated at the Jansenist College in Beauvais. With the success of his play *Andromaque* in 1667, Racine's true talent became obvious. He broke with Port Royal and was eventually appointed historiographer royal. Between 1667 and 1677, he produced seven tragedies and one comedy, and between 1689 and 1691, although by then he had virtually abjured playwriting, he produced two plays on Biblical themes. Racine claimed to be imitating only Euripides and Sophocles, but owed at least as much to his contemporaries, such as Corneille, proclaiming the bondage of man to instinct and the impossibility of satisfaction, as exemplified by his late tragedy, *Phèdre* (1691).

Hughes's version of this play (*Jean Racine: Phèdre*, a new version by Ted Hughes, Faber, 1998), first given a showing at Malvern, was put on in London by the Almeida Theatre Company in August 1998, directed by Jonathan Kent, with Diana Rigg as Phèdre and Toby Stephens as Hippolytus. That there was an earlier version by Robert Lowell, who also wrote a version of the *Oresteia*, is perhaps not without significance, since to some extent Hughes defines his own approach to translation in distinction to that of the American poet.

It seems that blank verse was not a viable option. Hughes was intent on conveying Racine's masterpiece as myth, rather than on seeking to represent the play in its literary-historical context, or by means of an updated or personalised transcription. The aim, evidently, was to make this neo-Classical tragedy accessible to a modern theatre audience, precluding the grandiloquence that characterises the source text.

Jonathan Kent, director of the London production of this translation, had proposed that Hughes translate *Medea*, but this was turned down. Kent later proposed *Phèdre*, and after a silence of two months received the translation complete. It seems, then, that Hughes set to work immediately, evidence of his commitment to the project. He translated directly from the French, working through the text himself, while probably referring to existing translations.

Phèdre is notoriously difficult to render successfully in English. In the preface to his own *Phaedra* (1960), Lowell talked of basing his metre on Dryden's and Pope's, but running his couplets on and avoiding inversions and alliterations. Lowell confessed that he inevitably echoed the style of the

English Restoration, 'both in ways that are proper and in my sometimes un-Racinian humour and bombast'. Tony Harrison (1975) transposed the play into an episode of British rule in India before the 1857 Mutiny.

The plot of *Phèdre* is as follows. Queen Phèdre has developed a passion for her stepson Hippolytus. He, however, is in love with Aricia, a captive princess whose brothers were slaughtered by King Theseus, Phèdre's husband and the father, by a former marriage, of Hippolytus. Theseus's assumed death allows Phèdre to confess her love for Hippolytus, a love that is not reciprocated. Then Theseus returns. Phèdre's nurse Oenone tells Theseus that Hippolytus has tried to betray him with Phèdre. Phèdre, learning of Hippolytus' love for Aricia, in her jealous rage, does not enlighten Theseus, who punishes Hippolytus. Eventually Hippolytus is killed by a sea monster, invoked by Theseus who has appealed to Neptune for vengeance. Phèdre takes a slow-working poison and confesses her guilt to Theseus, who survives, having been persuaded to take under his protection Hippolytus' betrothed, Aricia.

Excerpt 1

(*Act One. Théramène, Hippolytus' friend and counsellor, responds to Hippolytus' confession that he loves Aricia.*)

> My lord, once love has picked its man
> The gods cancel all his protestations.
> Theseus, trying to seal Aricia
> From the eyes of every man,
> Opened yours.
> Theseus' hatred for Aricia
> Surprised in you the opposite emotion.
> Aricia
> Has become irresistible – to you.
> But why shy from this passion?
> If you feel it – embrace it.
> Why forever tangle yourself, my lord,
> In these timid scruples?
> Hercules never hesitated.
> No heart ever begrudged the touch of Venus.
> You reject love
> But where would Hippolytus be
> If Antiope, your indomitable mother,
> Had not nursed that flame for your father?

In any case,
This pride which has given you such a name,
What does it amount to?
Admit it, things have changed.
You are not seen much lately, my lord,
Unperturbed, untouched, untouchable,
Hurtling along the sands in your chariot.
Or imitating the god of the ocean
Breaking a wild horse to amuse yourself.
And why are you heard so rarely these days
Scouring the woods with your hounds?
In your eye there's a new kind of fire –
Secretive, heavy, like an ailment.
You try to hide it. But it is killing you.
There is no hiding it. You are in love.
Is this Aricia?

Excerpt 2
(*Act One. Phèdre confesses to her nurse Oenone that she loves Hippolytus.*)

Suddenly he was there
Standing in front of me,
He had simply appeared –
Staring at me,
The man created
To destroy me.
Before I could grasp what I'd seen
I felt my face flame crimson – then go numb.
My whole body scorched – then icy sweat.
My eyes went dark.
I could not speak. I could hardly stand.
I knew then the goddess had found me –
The latest in the lineage that she loathes.
I had fallen
Into her furnace –
And I was trapped.
I tried to appease her.

My prayers were incessant.
I built her a shrine.
I spent half my wealth to decorate it.
From dawn to dusk I sacrificed beasts,
Searching their bodies for my sanity.
Futile placebo for a fatal illness!
And the incense I burned – equally futile!
All useless. Whenever I prayed
And bowed down to her image
I saw only his –
I adored only his.
Though I made the air shake with her titles
My whole heart and soul, my whole body
Worshipped only him – Hippolytus!
Then I began to avoid him.
But that was useless too.
I met him everywhere
In the face of his father –
Everywhere I saw him staring at me
Through his father's features.
So then I turned against him.
I turned against myself – to defend myself.
I forced myself
To make his life a misery. At last
I went the whole way – and drove him into exile.

Yes, I played the stepmother.
I pretended to hate him as my stepson.
As if his very presence poisoned me.
Night and day. Theseus had to hear that
And finally he relented.
So – his own father forced him to go.
Then I could breathe again, Oenone.
Once he'd gone the days flowed past me calmly.

I could conceal my anguish. I could be faithful.
I could even bear children.
But then, of a sudden,
All my precautions came to nothing.
Fate is inescapable.

Theseus brought me to Troezen.
And here, in Troezen,
I had to confront the one I had banished.
The first sight of him ripped my wounds wide open.
No longer a fever in my veins,
Venus has fastened on me like a tiger.
I know my guilt, and it terrifies me.
My own craving fills me with horror.
I detest my life.
I would have preferred to die
With what ought to be hidden cleanly hidden,
And my name intact,
But now you know everything
I will not regret it.
If only you will let me die quietly
And stop lashing me with these pointless reproaches,
And stop making such efforts to keep me alive.

Excerpt 3

(*Act Two. Hippolytus makes a declaration of love to Aricia.*)

I search your absence for you like a madman,
And yet I run from your presence.
Everywhere in the woods your image hunts me.
I try to escape you
But every shaft of sunlight,
Every night shadow
Sets you in front of me, surrounds me with you.
Everything competes to fling
The obstinate fool Hippolytus
Helpless at your feet.
All my studied care to preserve myself
Has brought me to this – I have lost myself,
I search – but I cannot find myself,
My bow, my spears, my chariot,
They beckon to me, I ignore them.
The breaking and taming of wild horses,
Everything the god of the sea taught me,

It is beyond me – I have forgotten it.
My own horses run wild –
They have forgotten my voice.
Nothing hears my voice but the forest –
The black echoing depth of the forest.
Yes, my love is a savage.
What raving words these are!
Maybe you blush to hear them.

Excerpt 4

(*Act Two. Phèdre confesseses her love for her stepson, Hippolytus.*)

I am in love.
But do not suppose for a second
I think myself guiltless
For loving you as I love you.
I have not
Indulged myself out of empty boredom.
I have not drunk this strychnine day after day
As an idle refreshment.
Wretched victim of a divine vengeance!
I detest myself
More than you can ever detest me.
You are right, the gods are watching me.
Yes, the same gods
Who have filled me with these horrible flames
That are killing me – as they have killed
All the women in my family.
[. . .]
O prince, I cannot speak to you
Of anything but you. Avenge yourself.
I am depraved. Act. Punish me.
Prove yourself the son of your father –
Rid the world of a monster!
The widow of King Theseus has dared
To fall in love with his son, Hippolytus.
This disgusting pest should be killed.
Look – my heart. Here.

Bury your sword here.
This heart is utterly corrupt.
It cannot wait to expiate its evil.
I feel it lifting to meet your stroke. Strike!
Or am I beneath your contempt?
Maybe my death seems too light a sentence.
Or are you apprehensive
That my polluted blood might foul your hand?
If your hands are reluctant, give me your sword.
Give me that sword!

Excerpt 5

(*Act Four. Hippolytus tries to defend himself against the injustice of Theseus' accusations. Much like Adonis in Shakespeare's 'Venus and Adonis', he prides himself on his purity – his mother, after all, being Antiope, an Amazon.*)

My mother's chastity was her fame.
There's not a drop of dissolute blood in me.
She formed me. Then Pitheus was my teacher.
The wisest, noblest, best man of his day.
I do not wish to boast but, my lord,
Above all other virtues, the one virtue
That I was born to, and have been bred up to,
Is hatred of this crime you charge me with.
My aversion to it is a legend.
Throughout Greece I am famed for just this.
Some say my rigour is so stubborn,
So severe, so blunt, they think it ugly,
Yet God knows the depth of my heart
Is pure as the blue sky! And still I hear you
Call me a hypocrite –

Excerpt 6
(*Act Four. Phèdre lacerates herself in self-disgust at her passion for her stepson.*)

> Oh God, what am I doing? What am I saying?
> I think I'm losing my senses.
> Me jealous? Me beg Theseus
> To avenge my jealousy? Implore my husband
> To remove my rival
> From my monstrous passion for his son?
> Everything I say makes my hair stand up.
> My life is so bloated with my crimes
> There's no room for another. I stink
> Of incest and deceit. And worse –
> My own hands are twitching
> To squeeze the life out of that woman,
> To empty that innocent blood out of her carcase
> And to smash her to nothing.
> Yet I stand here facing the sun.
> The light of heaven, my greatest ancestor,
> Is the father and ruler of the gods.
> The whole universe is full of my forebears.
> Where can I hide?
> I cannot hide even in Hell –
> My father, Minos, is the judge of the dead.
> There, the judgement favours nobody.
> He will be stupefied
> When I appear before him. His own daughter!
> Forced to confess to such crimes,
> So different and so many,
> Some of them perhaps
> Unknown even in Hell.

Excerpt 7
(*Act Five. Théramène reports the death of Hippolytus.*)

> We were hardly clear of the city gates
> And into the beach road, towards Mycenae.

Hippolytus was leading, in his chariot.
His bodyguards close round him. A sombre troop.
The prince was taciturn.
His mood made the mood of every man.
We all shared one dark thought and were silent.
No sound but the click of hooves and jingle of harness.
Those horses of his were strange.
Usually so bursting with spirits –
So headstrong, so eager to be off,
They need the constant touch of his voice and the reins
To hold them in – today they were listless.
He left the pace to them,
Letting the reins lie loose over their backs.
They hung their heads, they seemed preoccupied,
As if they were helping him, with their hanging heads,
To think what he was thinking.
I noticed it. It seemed very strange.
As I was watching that,
A suddenly skull-splitting roar,
An indescribable, terrible, tearing voice,
Like lightning flash and thunderclap together,
Made us all duck and cower.
It came out of the sea, as if the whole sea
Had bellowed.
And then, like an echo to it,
Another roaring groan, subterranean,
As if something that groaned were trying to scream,
Rolled through the earth under our feet.
The ground was bulging, jumping beneath us.
We were petrified and bewildered.
The horses' manes and tails flared on end.
And now I saw out at sea
A mountain of water boiling up,
Heaping higher,
Irrupting from under the horizon
And racing towards us,
Till it towered above us, seeming to hang.
And there, in slow motion,
It collapsed, a solid fall of thunder.

Quaking the bedrock. And out of it,
The foam cascading from a colossal body,
Came a beast –
Up the sand, with the fury
Of a supernatural existence.
Its head was one huge monster all to itself,
Like a bull's head, with bull's horns.
But from the shoulders backwards
The whole body was plated,
Humped and plated, the scales greeny yellow,
A nauseating colour, that sickened the eye.
And beyond the humped bulk of the body
Came scaled and lashing coils. Half bull, half dragon –
Mouth hanging open, like a cavern,
And bellowing, like a heavy surf
Exploding in a cavern.
The earth trembled, the air was thick with horror.
We breathed a mist of horror.

Euripides

Euripides (*c.*480–406 BC) was born near Athens and grew up during the period after the Persian War. He wrote about a hundred plays, only nineteen of which have survived – more, however, than the surviving plays of Aeschylus and Sophocles combined. Euripides is in some ways the forerunner of the modern psychological dramatist.

Ted Hughes began work on his version of the *Alcestis* in 1993. He seems to have made use of the translation by Philip Vellacott (*Alcestis and other Plays*, Penguin, 1959; first published in 1933). It is likely that he also consulted a version by the late William Arrowsmith (New York and London, 1974). Barrie Rutter, director of Yorkshire's Northern Broadsides Theatre Company, to whom Hughes offered the play in August 1998, directed the first production.

Euripides' fondness for rhetorical speeches makes his work less accessible to theatre audiences in our day than that of the other Greek tragedians – the rhetorically inclined Seneca to a certain extent recalls Euripides in this respect – but this aspect of his work may also account for Hughes's interest in it. The contrast between grandiosity of setting and highly personal content was one that may have appealed, challenging the conventions of discursive realistic theatre. As Keith Sagar points out in an essay (2001) on *Alcestis*, Hughes's version of the play adds a great deal to Euripides. Death's speech, for instance, is wholly an invention of Hughes.

In a letter to Hughes in September 1998, the Northern Broadsides director Barry Rutter writes: 'I love the craziness of mourning and pantomime combined; can only think Euripides was gleefully being impudent in entering it as a Satyr slot.' It seems clear that Hughes produced the version on his own initiative rather than in response to a suggestion or commission. A review (www.Mytholmroyd.net/tedhughes/alcestis2.html) describes the Northern Broadsides production as having been 'superbly acted by a cast who had real rather than stage northern accents, dispelling the southern, cultural notion that great literature can only be performed by actors using the dialect of the south-east'. It seems fair to suppose also that Hughes was pleased to entrust this, his last substantial work and one of universal range, to a company from his home county.

The plot is as follows. King Admetos of Thessaly is to die, but his wife Alcestis opts to take his place, his father Pheres and his mother having refused to do so. The god Apollo begs Death to have mercy. Then Admetos' friend Heracles (Hercules), son of Zeus, appears. He wrestles with Death and succeeds in bringing Alcestis back. What has been an almost unbearable tragedy ends in a paean of joy and thanksgiving.

Excerpt 1
(*Admetos reflects on Orpheus' attempt to rescue his dead wife.*)

> I find myself
> Thinking about Orpheus – in the thick of all this.
> Thinking of the impossible.
> How he went down there,
> Into the underworld, the dead land,
> With his guitar and his voice –
> He rode the dark road
> On the thumping of a guitar,
> A horse of music.
> He wrapped himself in his voice,
> Deathproof, a voice of asbestos,
> He went
> Down and down and down.
> You remember –
> He went for his dead wife
> And he nearly got her.
> Death let her go – on one condition.
> Orpheus almost saved her. But –
> He loved her too much, too helplessly.
> He made a little mistake.
> He made it out of love.
> A tiny error – unthinking –
> A glance. Think of it. Only a backward glance.
> And he had done what he should never have done.
> At the crucial moment.
> He lost her.
> Horrible!

Excerpt 2

*(A maidservant describes Alcestis' preparations for death and her
concern for her two children.)*

> [. . .] And she prayed.
> 'Goddess:
> You who have blessed my house,
> Today I am going into the earth.
> By this evening
> I shall be nothing in the dark nothing of death.
> This is the last time I shall kneel here
> To ask you anything.
> Goddess,
> Protect my children, be their mother,
> And guide them
> Into strong marriages.
> And let them live their lives to the utmost day,
> Do not let them be plucked, like me,
> Before they are ripe for falling.'

Excerpt 3

(Admetos rails at Death.)

> Words!
> Don't you see what has happened?
> She dreamed of the great black bird
> With no eyes in its sockets
> That flew at her, and pecked her –
> Now I have to act like a man in control
> And manage the funeral.
>
> Friends, I am thankful you are here.
> You know what we must do now.
> We must sing
> In defiance of this loathsome god
> Who collects our bodies
> With anger at our reluctance,
> Like a debt collector.

But first let the year of mourning begin.
Let the people be with me in my sorrow.
Let every head be shaved.
Let every garment be black.
Let the cavalry
Crop the manes and tails of the horses.
Throughout the city
Let every stringed instrument be unstrung.
Let every flute lie breathless.

Never in my life
Shall I bury anyone
I loved so much, or who loved me more.
She died for me. Let her be honoured
As she deserves.

Excerpt 4

(*Heracles, not knowing that Alcestis is already dead, argues with Admetos, trying to persuade him to take heart.*)

HERACLES
    I heard. You were doomed to die early.
    She offered to take your place.
    The whole world knows the story.

ADMETOS
    In that case, Heracles, don't you see –
    If she is doomed to die
    How can I think of her as alive?

HERACLES
    But any one of us can be killed tomorrow.
    We don't ruin today with worrying about it.
    Death can come in a twinkling, any second.
    Up to that second every second is precious,
    Precious, precious life.
    Death has to be ignored.
    Then when it comes – mourn. Acknowledge it.
    But not before it comes.

Excerpt 5

(A Servant voices a general anxiety that entertaining obstreperous guests such as Heracles is what now lies in store for them all.)

So while they bury Alcestis
We have to humour this – whatever he is!
A wild man of the woods,
A mountain man, brought up by bears –
This guzzler and devourer.
He wanted to go to the funeral.
Alcestis cared for us all,
She mothered us all.
The King had his weakness.
He can't quite believe
He deserves his good fortune.
His temper is not so reliable.
He's a bit of a touchy bull.
Alcestis kept him calm.
She protected us from him.
But what will happen now she's gone?
I think this new guest is a sign
Of what it's going to be like.
If this dangerous buffoon
Is the kind he likes about him –
The signs are very bad.

Excerpt 6

(Heracles describes how he will rescue Alcestis from Death.)

I must hurry.
Death will be there already
Lapping up the blood that pours
From the sacrificed beasts.
Then while the mourners wail
And try to convert the pain of grief
Into physical wounds on their own bodies,
Death will bend over her.

He'll embrace her.
He'll plant his cold kiss on her dry lips –

Then he will feel, as he bends there,
My arms around his neck.
If I'm too late, no matter,
I shall go down through the earth –
And if I fail to overtake them
I shall penetrate
The palace of the God of Hell
And his poor unfortunate Queen, Persephone.
They will not refuse me.
I shall pluck Alcestis, like a stalk of asphodel,
From the tossing crowd of new shadows,
And I shall hand her back to Admetos,
This lord of hospitality
Who made me so welcome, even in his worst hour.

Excerpt 7
(*Admetos laments the loss of his wife.*)

This house! This horrible empty box!
A huge grave.
In it, one huge wound – that took the life
And is now cold.
A numbed mouth with swollen lips
Left behind by a pain too huge to utter.
Pain – dark pain.
Instead of the light – pain.
No refuge anywhere in me
From this fire, this huge dark single flame,
That caresses my whole body.
I think of cool soil,
A mask over my face,
A weight of stillness over my body,
A darkness
In which she lies next to me – her lips
Maybe only an inch from my lips.

Forever.
[. . .]
The mind tries to be its own doctor.
But every thought of her
Rips off the dressings, sets the blood flowing afresh.
We should never have married.
Men who have never married
Keep their nerves inside their own skin.
The nerves of the married man,
His very entrails, all his arteries
Are woven into the body of his wife –
And into the bodies of his children.
Let the groom beware.
Yes, and let the bride beware too.

Excerpt 8
(*Admetos proclaims the happier lot of his wife, in death.*)

My wife is happy.
Life is agony and she is free of it.
What greater good fortune can there be
Than to escape the worst that life can bear –
As she has escaped it.
I have to face it.
I dodge my fate. I who should be dead
Now have to face this life.
At last I understand what that means.
How can I enter my own house?
Who will greet me there?
Her empty chair. The imprint of her body
On our bed. And the children
Crying for their mother.

And where else can I go? Wherever I go
I shall see weddings,
Dancing excited women and girls –
I shall see her friends among them.
I shall feel like an animal

With a fatal wound –
Wanting only to crawl off into a hole.

And what will be said about me?
Everywhere the same:
'There he goes.
How can he shame to stay alive?
That coward
Who was so afraid of death
When his father and mother refused
To die in his place he cursed them.
When he saw death coming, like an arrow,
He dodged behind his wife.
He let her die for him, to save his life.'
Don't ask me to live!
When every man or woman who knows my story
Can deal me this wound, and will deal it.
Even if they do not say it, they will think it.
How can I live with this?

Excerpt 9
(*Heracles has rescued Alcestis from Death and returns her to Admetos, pretending at first that she is a woman that he has won in a contest.*)

HERACLES
    She is yours, Admetos.
    I will not hand her to anyone but you.

ADMETOS
    Let her go in alone. I will not touch her.

HERACLES
    Your right hand. This one. Lead her –

ADMETOS
    This is neither the time nor the place for your strength.

HERACLES
    It is for you to be strong.
    My strength is the strength you are rejecting.

Welcome your guest. Close her hand in yours.
Look at her – you are not beheading a Gorgon
Who will turn you to stone.
You hold her?

ADMETOS

Yes, I hold her hand.

HERACLES

Protect her, Admetos. Cherish her.
And one day you will say
Heracles, son of Zeus, was a noble guest.
And now Admetos, look at her. Look at her face.
Tell us if she resembles Alcestis
As you thought she did.
Forget your sorrows. Look at happiness.

(*Admetos lifts the Woman's veil.*)

ADMETOS

You gods in heaven!
Give me the words!
Heracles, have you hypnotised me
To see what I cannot believe?

HERACLES

No hypnosis, Admetos.
This is your wife, Alcestis.

ADMETOS

Or a ghost? Conjured up for a moment.
You can do anything, Heracles
But don't trick me.

HERACLES

I am your friend, remember.
The son of Zeus, not a conjuror.

ADMETOS

I buried her today, Alcestis?

HERACLES
This is your true and only wife, Alcestis.

ADMETOS
Can I embrace her? Will she speak to me?

HERACLES
She is yours.
All you had thought you had lost – she is here.

ADMETOS
Alcestis!

HERACLES
May no watching god be jealous.

ADMETOS
Heracles!
Your labours, your entire glorious life
Are nothing to this.
May Zeus your father
Guard your life
As you have given me mine,
As you have restored my wife's life to her.
But how did it happen?

HERACLES
I fought with the God of Death.

Excerpt 10
(*The play ends on a note almost of triumphant optimism, in the Hughes version.*)

CHORUS 3
And now
See how God has accomplished
What was beyond belief.

CHORUS 1
Let this give man hope.

Alexander Pushkin

Ted Hughes's last known poem is a translation: a version of 'The Prophet' by Alexander Pushkin (1799–1837), first published in the *Daily Telegraph* on 9 January 1999, Valentina Polukhina and I having provided him with the literal version, some historical notes and notes on the prosody. He had been invited to contribute to *After Pushkin* (1999), edited by Elaine Feinstein, to mark the bicentenary of Pushkin's birth, and had chosen 'The Prophet', a poem, apparently, which he had for some time wished to translate. The political implications of this piece, based on Isaiah 6:1–13, are clear enough, but it was perhaps the exaltation of the visionary's role that drew Hughes, as well as the shamanistic character of Pushkin's treatment of this theme.

The transliteration of the Russian source text was accompanied by an ad-verbum or literal translation and a literate version, to be used in conjunction with the latter (see Appendix 15). That Hughes transformed the given texts is evident from the last six lines, the literal version of which reads: 'I lay like a corpse in the desert, / And the voice of God called out to me: / "Arise, prophet, and see, and hear, / Carry out my will, / And passing by sea and land, / Burn the hearts of people with the word."' These lines were translated by Hughes as follows:

> I lay on stones like a corpse.
> There God's voice came to me:
> 'Stand, Prophet, you are my will.
> Be my witness. Go
> Through all seas and lands. With the Word
> Burn the hearts of the people.'

Hughes's interest in Pushkin dates from at least 1964, when he wrote in a review of a selection of Pushkin's letters (see 'Opposing Selves', *Winter Pollen*): 'Pushkin gives a peculiar impression of being something utterly different from his fellow-Russians – not just a genius, but different in kind, like some sort of changeling from outer space.' He sees Pushkin as both the sophisticated, Frenchified aristocrat and the solitary sufferer, a kind of spiritual outlaw or primitive ['he liked to think of his private monopoly of primitive African passion']. In the same year, 1964, came Nabokov's translation of and commentary on 'Eugene Onegin', much admired by Hughes. When he used the somewhat problematical term 'primitive', perhaps what he also had in mind was the elemental nature of this poem, with its Biblical associations and its rehearsal of the shamanistic-Christian journey through death and resurrection. Hughes's interest in shamanism is well known and much of his own work bears witness to it. 'The Prophet' recalls shamanistic practices, even to the insertion of something rock-like in the to-be-resurrected body: 'He split my chest with a blade, / Wrenched my heart from its hiding, And into the open wound / Dropped a flaming coal.'

The Prophet

Crazed by my soul's thirst
Through a dark land I staggered.
And a six-winged seraph
Halted me at a crossroads.
With fingers of dream
He touched my eye-pupils.
My eyes, prophetic, recoiled
Like a startled eaglet's.
He touched my ears
And a thunderous clangour filled them,
The shudderings of heaven,
The huge wingbeat of angels,
The submarine migration of sea-reptiles
And the burgeoning of the earth's vine.
He forced my mouth wide,
Plucked out my own cunning
Garrulous evil tongue,
And with bloody fingers
Between my frozen lips
Inserted the fork of a wise serpent.
He split my chest with a blade,
Wrenched my heart from its hiding,
And into the open wound
Dropped a flaming coal.
I lay on stones like a corpse.
There God's voice came to me:
'Stand, Prophet, you are my will.
Be my witness. Go
Through all seas and lands. With the Word
Burn the hearts of the people.'

Appendices

APPENDIX 1   Ted Hughes on translation

As can be seen from his programme note written for Poetry International 1967, which was directed by himself and Patrick Garland, Ted Hughes believed in the permeability of linguistic, cultural and political borders, and in the ability, in any case, of poetry to transcend these. It is this belief which underlies his validation of 'literal' translation, as he saw it, and which informed also the early policy of the editors of the journal Modern Poetry in Translation *(1965–), a project conceived of by Hughes some years before. The first editorial, excerpted below, is combative enough, but seeks to appear mild, in an attempt not to antagonise those who held very different views. Hughes's own need or desire for literal versions, which he felt brought him as close as may be to the source texts is clear from the editorial to MPT 3: 'The very oddity and struggling dumbness of word for word versions is what makes our own imagination jump.'*

Poetry International 1967: Programme Note by Ted Hughes

In this Festival, poets from nine different countries will take part [these included Patrick Kavanagh, Stephen Spender, W. H. Auden, Anthony Hecht, Ingeborg Bachmann, Robert Graves, Charles Olson, Hugh MacDiarmid, Allen Ginsberg, William Empson, Anne Sexton, John Berryman, Yehuda Amichai, Pablo Neruda, Yves Bonnefoy, Hans Magnus Enzensberger; the Russian poet Bella Akhmadulina was also invited but was not permitted to attend]. The idea for such a gathering was suggested by the great and growing public for poetry which is making itself felt in London just as surely as in Moscow and New York. However rootedly-national in detail it may be, poetry is less and less the prisoner of its own language. It is beginning to represent, as an ambassador, something far greater than itself. Or perhaps it is only now being heard for what, among other things, it is – a Universal language of understanding, coherent behind the many languages, in which we can all hope to meet.

We now give more serious weight to the words of a country's poets than to the words of its politicians – though we know the latter may interfere more drastically with our lives. Religions, ideologies, mercantile competition divide us. The essential solidarity of the very diverse poets of the world, besides being a mysterious fact, is one we can be thankful for, since its terms are exclusively those of love, understanding and patience. It is one of the few spontaneous guarantees of possible unity that mankind can show, and the revival of an appetite for poetry is like a revival of an appetite for all man's saner possibilities, and a revulsion from the materialist cataclysm of recent years and the worse ones which the difference of nations threatens for the years ahead.

The idea of global unity is not new, but the absolute necessity of it has only just arrived, like a sudden radical alteration of the sun, and we shall have to adapt or disappear. If the various nations are ever to make a working synthesis of their ferocious contradictions, the plan of it and the temper of it will be created in spirit before it can be formulated or accepted in political fact. And it is in poetry that we can refresh our hopes that such a unity is occupying people's imaginations everywhere, since poetry is the voice of spirit and imagination and all that is potential, as well as of the healing benevolence that used to be the privilege of the gods.

It is in this belief, that a gathering of the inspired poets of nine different countries is timely and amounts to much more than a great cultural event, that this Festival is planned.

Modern Poetry in Translation (No. 1, 1965): Editorial (excerpt)

(This was unsigned, and written jointly by Hughes and the editor of the present volume. The views and intentions expressed are those of Hughes.]

The type of translation we are seeking can be described as literal, though not literal in a strict or pedantic sense. Though this may seem at first suspect, it is more apposite to define our criteria negatively, as literalness can only be a deliberate tendency, not a dogma. We feel that as soon as devices extraneous to the original are employed for the purpose of recreating its 'spirit', the value of the whole enterprise is called in question. Also 'imitations' like Robert Lowell's, while undeniably beautiful, are the record of the effect of one poet's imagination on another's. They may help in the appreciation of the original, they may simply obscure it. In any case, the original becomes strangely irrelevant. Poetry inevitably loses hugely in translation, but those purists who claim that it is precisely 'the poetry' which is lost are speaking as though 'the poetry' were some separable ingredient, some additive like the whitening agent in a detergent. We feel that enough of the whole is preservable in some, though by no means in all, poetry.

Modern Poetry in Translation (No. 3, Spring 1967): Editorial (excerpt)

In the present unusually fertile period of translations, it is right that there should be plenty of theories in the air – the more opposed the better, in our opinion. Nevertheless, after our experience as editors of this paper, we feel more strongly than ever that the first ideal is literalness, insofar as the original is what we are curious about. The very oddity and struggling dumbness of word for word versions is what makes our own imagination jump. A man who has something really serious to say in a language of which he knows only a few words, manages to say it far more convincingly and effectively than any interpreter, and in translated poetry it is the first-hand contact – however fumbled and broken – with that man and his seriousness which we want. The minute we gloss his words, we have more or less what he said but we have lost him. We are ringing changes – amusing though they may be – on our familiar abstractions, and are no longer reaching through to what we have not experienced before, which is alive and real.

The only justification, it would seem to us, for anything but the most literal of translations, is [i] in those rare cases where the original poetry somehow makes an original and interesting poet of the translator who is not otherwise a poet, as with Arthur Waley, and [ii] where the translator already is an inter-esting and original poet in his own right, and in his 'versions' we are glad to get more of him, extensions and explorations of his possibilities, as in the extraordinary Heine and Rilke translations in Lowell's *Imitations*. The great mass of translation is neither of these. It pretends to a parallel, or a recreation which effectively misguides and deceives us in our attempt to re-imagine the original, and is of no interest in itself. The most that can be said for it is that it excites our curiosity and holds our attention for a few minutes and exercises our detective talents – before it simply bores us, and it is not so harmless as newspaper riddles.

Modern Poetry in Translation (1982): Introduction

At this stage in *MPT*'s long career, one feels tempted to look back over the unique tidal wave of poetry translation that swept through English (and through the other chief Western languages) in the 'sixties and early 'seventies. Where did it come from and what happened to it?

That boom in the popular sales of translated modern poetry was without precedent. Though it reflected only one aspect of the wave of mingled energies that galvanised those years with such extremes, it was fed by almost all of them. From other standpoints, other aspects might seem more significant. There are diagnoses to be drawn from the mass epidemic of infatuation with hallucinogenic drugs, the sudden opening to all of the worlds of Eastern mys-tical practice and doctrine, particularly of various forms of Buddhism, the mass craze of Hippie ideology, the revolt of the young, the Pop music of the Beatles and their generation, the Walpurgisnacht of new psychotherapies. From yet other standpoints, all these must appear as the natural but minor harmonics of the real historical event – the shock-wave consequences of modern physics working through the old, anachronistic human system, and materialising in the new bomb and the imminent end of the world, which was dramatised and magnified by the confrontation of Russia and the United States. The stage was being set, in those days, by our dawning realisation – it had taken time – of what Hitler and Stalin had actually made of mankind, as if they had revealed it of ourselves, as if there had been some sort of mutation in humanity, though history reassured us, in depressing confirmation, a refreshed understanding of the old evidence, that we had always shared these weaknesses, just as Hiroshima, Nagasaki and the war in Vietnam circumstantially confirmed that the guilt was indeed ours. It is easy to forget, in the crowded perspective of recent history, that these realisations took form as a shocking novelty. I call it the setting of a stage, but it could feel more like biological inevitability, an evolutionary first phase, an inescapable preparation for some final human confession and apocalypse. That historical moment might well be seen, by a detached Spenglerian, as a development from the spiritual plane, an unfolding from inwards, a millennial change in the Industrial West's view of reality that had roots far back in time. But all the immediate circumstances of it were, to say the least, unacceptable. And when the whole burden was touched off, as it was, by factors that seem almost coincidental, one can understand how the resulting euphoric madness came to have such pathos, and such universal appeal. It was a forlorn adolescent attempt to establish *agape* as a world republic. We were all taken unawares by a decade that became in many ways a poetic image simply for youth, which had behind it the magical power of sexual awakening, and the archaic biological imperative, to love and embrace everybody, especially those with foreign genes, before it is too late.

The factors that touched off this conflagration were of course, the surge of economic prosperity that rose out of the late 'fifties, as the West recovered from the Second World War, and the emergence of all Western Countries, and indeed of all the countries of the world, from the Ice Age of that war and the Dark Age that had preceded it. That re-awakening of the world's countries, to themselves and to each other, after such nightmare experiences, was a stirring thing to live through. If the Modern Age burst from its crib in the 1914–18 war, it came to consciousness of itself in the 'sixties. It was forced to consciousness. One can easily understand the suddenness of the need to communicate, to exchange dreams and revelations and brainwaves, to find a shared humanity on the level of the heart. The flux of poetry translation followed inevitably. And not only on the level of the heart. The translation of poetry became important, almost political business. The political role of poetry in Russia certainly had something to do with this. In one sense, the transmission from Russia, which began with *Dr Zhivago*, was the carrier wave of the whole poetry translation phenomenon. As the alter ego of the Soviet global threat, modern Russian poetry can be seen lifting poetry translation to the crest of excitement. Through this circuit, the mood of doom found a strange kind of hope in the poetry of other nations, or perhaps simply in the poetry of humanity felt as a whole, as a single threatened creature. And perhaps this explains why poetry for those brief years became central to the exploration of drugs, of Buddhism, of imaginative systems from the childhood of the race, of the music and liberties of the young. One feels that only a giant collapse, a bankruptcy, a momentary utter fatigue of all other civilised promises, could have let this happen. It was indeed a confession of sorts, a moment of psychic nakedness. Obviously it could not last. Mankind readjusted, the ego recovered its resilience. Even if the money had not run out, it could not have lasted. As it was, in quite a short time, the main landmarks of the world's modern poetry became accessible to all, the glamorous, stormy affair with Russia entered its grim, realistic years of marriage, the Beatles generation began to grow deaf and grey, and to worry about its children.

Throughout all the confusions of that period runs one tenacious band. It was established in the late 'fifties before the mounting potential showed any very visible portents, and it is still unbroken now the uproar is well past. This band consisted and consists of the working translators. The best of them continue to be active – and most of them are still comparatively young. And though their popular audience has been absorbed back into the landscape, and publishers are more and more reluctant to cooperate, some of their finest achievements have appeared quite recently, and others are only now, in 1982, moving towards publication.

Probably one's own generation always seems to have played a key role of some sort, so I may be wrong in my impression that the main work of translating poetry was done – was certainly initiated – by the generation born five years or so either side of 1930.

In 1960, before things began to move, before the Beatles had lifted their voice, the translation of poetry seemed to lie in the hands of a few enterprising individuals who were merely following their own bent, as poets here and there always have done, unearthing from other languages what they couldn't find lying around them in their own. Robert Bly was setting up The Sixties Press. But if you were aware of him at all, his rallying calls for recruits to the cause of Vallejo, Trakl, and others, sounded as much like a last stand as (what it was) the beach-head of an invasion. W. S. Merwin seemed to be toiling away in the traditional wage-earning task – translating Juvenal and Mediaeval French as readily as Eluard and Neruda – rather than embarking, as he was, on the immense map of adventurous foreign explorations which he has since filled in with such marvellous detail. At that time, one's own fascination with what they were doing carried no feeling of what was on its way. One was too aware, perhaps, of the solid wall of dismissal (and derision) that the poetic and critical canon of the 'fifties presented to such alien texts. But when the wave arrived, and the passionate international affair commenced, suddenly almost all the poets of this generation found that the dull isolations of the 'fifties had been imposed on them, and that they were all interested in the same thing: translating the poetry of other languages. Everything happened then at heady speed. And it was curious to watch those somewhat war-time utility, old-fashioned personalities (the last of the old order) casting off ten years in style of dress and behaviour and taste in music, and immersing in the headlong element of joyful freedoms that had snatched up their translations (and everybody felt the pull). No doubt they were fore-runners anyway, a little ahead of their times, and naturally susceptible. In the long run, some of them became leaders of a sort, and took further than anybody else the determination to transform themselves and to enter the new world thoroughly adjusted – an attempt as evident in Merwin and Bly as it is in Ginsberg.

As these names suggest, the Americans performed the tendencies more whole-heartedly, but in the end the overlap of curiosity was pretty well complete, among English translators and American, though with a characteristic – and revealing – difference in their preferred fields of attention.

This seemed clear, at least, when we launched the first issue of *Modern Poetry in Translation*. Daniel Weissbort and myself had been talking for years about a magazine of this sort. In the end, as the boom neared its peak, with publishers calling for more, and almost every poet we knew busy with translation, it seemed easier to let the magazine take off than to keep it grounded. The sheer pressure of material forced the issue. Even so, in that maiden flight our material was of a particular kind.

From the start we saw our editorship as something like an airport for incoming translations, an agency for discovering new foreign poets, and new translators, who then, if their qualifications were right, might pass inland to more permanent residences in published books. We had a general notion of making familiar to English readers the whole range of contemporary possibilities in poetry – in so far as translation can convey any idea of such things. We weren't beyond the hope of influencing our own writers in a productive way. We even toyed with the fantasy of sending to every known poet – offering to their curiosity – a free copy of each issue. Acquaintance with the diverse poetries of the modern world, we felt, couldn't be bad, even if it only helped to confirm home-grown virtues. That fantasy evaporated with the first bills, but it was partly responsible for our format – a flimsy newspaper (the first issue was on ricepaper) that would never seem to demand more than a cursory scanning, and wouldn't much resist being thrown away. Functional, current, disposable – such were our key words. And our ambition was to build up, eventually, the complete picture.

The same approach determined the large amount of material we tried to pack in. We had some hope of shifting the contents from the fine arts category – and the highly-developed resistance it meets – to that of a bulk commodity, almost like news. We would have liked to hurry the response of our readers from insular wariness in face of the foreign object (we always thought of an English audience) towards a casual, easy acceptance of the world's medley of poetic dialects. These ideas were probably indefensible, and they certainly lacked market research, but they did crystallise a vital opportunity in the air of the time, and they served our real purpose – they were effectively creative in that they helped us to get the current flowing in volume, and kept it flowing with a momentum that occasionally moved large freight. The reservoir of material seemed inexhaustible – more like a sea than a reservoir, a living, evolving, circulating sea. And since we proposed to assemble each issue from the poetry of a single country, or of two or three related countries, we set out with what was virtually an infinitely long-term plan.

This wide-open hospitality to all Modern Poetry, which was the overall character of our policy, meant that the decisive thing came to be our personal taste in poetic quality, and in style of translation. Later on (after I had withdrawn from the co-editorship, which I did so there should be no embarrassing mistake about who was doing all the hard work), it was Daniel Weissbort's taste alone, or, occasionally, that of some guest editor. But in all the years since, Daniel Weissbort has held to the guiding principles we started with, refining them on the way in the perennial debate concerning the various virtues of the various methods of translation. Since our only real motive in publishing was our own curiosity in contemporary foreign poetry, we favoured the translations that best revealed the individuality and strangeness of the original. This usually meant a translation that interposed the minimum of the reflexes and inventions of the translator. The exemplary demonstration of this appears in Shelley's note to his translation of the opening chorus of Goethe's *Faust*. We were happily resigned, that is, to all the losses sustained by the most literal translation of the verbal sense. This method can have some drastic results: where the original poem's centre of gravity, so to speak, lies in the verbal texture, the poem can easily disappear completely. (Pushkin is the famous case of how all-important the verbal texture can be.) But 'the most literal' covers a wide range between denotative and connotative extremes. Ideally, we would have liked to see at least some poems translated with the concern for both extremes served as meticulously and flexibly as in Bleek's translation of Bushman lore – though we understood the limited appeal of anything so raw and strange unless it has the guarantee behind it of a literary personality as solid, say, as Beckett's. We tried to avoid translators who claimed to produce a 'parallel equivalent' of some original's unique verbal texture. It seemed to us, in our purism, that a 'parallel equivalent' in the way of imagery, evocative effects, rhyme schemes etc., had to be a new thing, quite different from what we were after. However fine it might be in itself, in relation to the original it could only be the crudest of analogies, with the added crime that it seduced honest curiosity with a charming counterfeit. What we were looking for, naturally, was the best of both worlds, and as in the Bushman lore of Bleek we occasionally found it in the work of very modest poets. Most often, oddly enough, but perhaps inevitably, we found the closest thing to it in translations made by poets whose first language was not English, or by scholars who did not regard themselves as poets. Among the still-readable survivors of the translations made in the last twenty years, a surprising number have been made by such people. Our high principles were all very well in theory, and as touchstones, but in practice, of course, we had to compromise, and were quite ready to if the results seemed to us provisionally worthwhile.

What finally overwhelmed us into publishing our first issue was the translated work of a group of poets who seemed to us revelatory. A little earlier, Al Alvarez had brought back from Eastern Europe poems by Miroslav Holub (Czechoslovakia) and by Zbigniew Herbert (Poland). About the same time, Daniel Weissbort found poems by Vasko Popa (Serbia) and Yehuda Amichai (Israel). I came across poems by János Pilinszky (Hungary).

Over the next years, other poets – Celan, Różewicz – would emerge through translation to join them, but these first few impressed us as a totally new phenomenon. And it is interesting to note, in passing, that the Holub was translated by a Czech (George Theiner), Herbert by a Pole (Czesław Miłosz), Vasko Popa, in the translations we first saw, by himself (and Anne Pennington, who later translated him so miraculously, regarded herself as a scholar with no claim to being a poet or even a versifier). Yehuda Amichai seemed good in any translation, but the best, the most touching and haunting, were by himself. And we found Pilinszky in translations made by the exiled Hungarian poet János Csokits. To complete this list, Różewicz was eventually translated by a fellow-Pole, Adam Czerniawski, and Celan by Michael Hamburger. The 1930 generation of American and English translators, in fact, had very little to do with this particular invasion, except in giving them an appreciative welcome (and except insofar as Michael Hamburger was one of the earliest, as he has proved one of the most gifted and productive).

That group of poets all belonged to the 1920 generation, the generation that came of age during the war, and they belonged together in an obvious way. They seemed to us to be the serious voice of that historical moment. It was common in those days to hear how all poetry had died in Auschwitz, but theirs seemed not only to have taken full account of it and survived it, but to have created a new moral being out of the experience, already adapted to the worst imaginable future. And all these poets shared another characteristic: in literal translation, their work made English poems of great freshness, force and truth. Whatever the verbal texture of the originals might be, evidently their real centre of gravity was in something else, within the images and the pattern of ideas and attitudes. They also enjoyed, no doubt, a lucky combination of translators. But for us, as I have said, they more than justified the launching of *MPT*. They made it inevitable.

Since then, Daniel Weissbort has steered the magazine through 44 issues. The collected volumes now make a weighty Encyclopedia of Modern Poetry in Translation – a mine that has not been neglected by anthologists, researchers, publishers or poets. Just what we hoped it would be. Meanwhile the translators go on working at what is now a great series of naturalised poetic monuments. However fashionable support may come and go in the future, there seems to be no reason why that should not go on.

APPENDIX 2 *Bardo Thödol*

*The description of the process of death has apparently no direct connection with W. Y. Evans-Wentz's translation (*The Tibetan Book of the Dead: The After-Death Experiences of the *Bardo Plane, according to Lama Kazi Dawa-Samdup's English Rendering, compiled and edited by W. Y. Evans-Wentz, 3rd edition, Oxford University Press, 1957). The prayer to the Buddhas and Bodhisattvas, on the other hand, draws on the prayers or 'Paths of Good Wishes', given as an Appendix to the Evans-Wentz volume (p.197 ff.: 'there are thirteen folios of rituals and prayers . . . which all professional readers of the* Bardo Thödol *must know, usually from memory, and apply as needed . . .'). Below is an excerpt from this translation, on which Hughes drew to produce his own composite version of these prayers.*

'O ye Compassionate Ones, ye possess the wisdom of understanding, the love of compassion, the power of [doing] divine deeds and of protecting, in incomprehensible measure. Ye Compassionate Ones such-and-such a person is passing from this world to the world beyond. He is leaving this world. He is taking a great leap . . .'

[The Obeisances]

> To the Divine Body of Truth, the Incomprehensible,
>> Boundless Light;
> To the Divine Body of Perfect Endowment, Who are the
>> Lotus and the Peaceful and the Wrathful Deities;
> To the Lotus-born Incarnation, Padma Sambhava, Who is
>> the Protector of all sentient beings;
> To the Gurus, the Three Bodies, obeisance.

APPENDIX 3 Mário de Sá Carneiro

Ted Hughes to Helder and Suzette Macedo

I'm sending you these 'translations' of the Sá Carneiro, because I would like to hear what you think of my somewhat free manner of anglicising them. The long piece is [. . .] effective I thought, and where I've altered it I'm not sure I've improved it. But the other two I changed – in detail – quite severely, as you'll see. I enjoyed doing these two very much, so much so that if you would 'English' – roughly but as literally as possible (even to the word order), about a dozen, perhaps we could get a group ready for a magazine. But you might not like my verbal presumptions – though I'm sure the original looks much more bizarre.

　　[. . .]

The rougher & more literal the translations are the more suggestive to me they are. Just word by word transcription would be ideal.

APPENDIX 4 Helder Macedo

Suzette Macedo's literal, sent to Hughes

> When the mirror breaks
> there is still the face
> impersonal and precise
> to be unbound
>
> When the mirror breaks
> we are face to face
> facing one another
> more than ourselves
>
> when the mirror breaks
> my love
> let us search
> so deeply in each other
>
> that our bodies
> can reconstruct
> as a record against death
> the mortal essence that defined them.

Suzette Macedo to Daniel Weissbort, 19 August 2004

The parenthetical bits are . . . Ted's queries/comments. His draft translation is very different, with some odd departures and additions, e.g. 'face to face' in stanza two becomes 'Your nakedness and / Mine whisper / Together against us'; the image of hands holding torches or flames in the last stanza is nowhere in the original, though it may have suggested itself to him, because of the idea of an 'essence' raised against death.

Hughes to Helder and Suzette Macedo (c.1962)

First of all, about your poems. I liked them very much, particularly the love poems [. . .] I'm afraid I distorted your originals somewhat. Your poetry includes or indicates meanings that can't be nailed down with words, whereas the great characteristic (and great limitation) of my language is to nail things down. This is what I made of no III. I feel I've spoiled the original to make a more concrete but less suggestive poem ['When the mirror is broken open', see above].

 The last verse is a remote & mutilated paraphrase of your meaning, but it is a sort of metaphorical version of it. Anyway that gives you some idea of what I did. As you see, I kept mainly, Suzette, your translation – which was often felicitous.

APPENDIX 5   Ferenc Juhász

Kenneth McRobbie version

> Her own son the mother called
> from afar crying
> her own son the mother called
> from afar crying,
> she went before the house, from there calling
> her hair's full knot she loosed,
> with it the dusk wove a dense quivering
> veil, a precious cloak down to her ankles . . .

David Wevill version

> The mother called to her own son,
> cried from far away,
> the mother called to her own son,

cried from far away,
went to the front of the house: from there she cried,
unwound her heavy knot of hair
dusk wove to a shimmering bride's veil
that flowed down to her ankles . . .

APPENDIX 6 Yehuda Amichai

Amichai's English literal of his poem 'Letter of Recommendation'

[. . .]

I remember my father waking me up
for early prayers. He did it caressing
my forehead, not tearing the blanket away.
Since then I love him even more.
And because of this
let him be woken up
gently and with love
on the Day of Resurrection.

[*Hughes made minimal changes in the draft given him by the author. In general, he does not shrink from a certain foreignness; indeed, he often seems to embrace it. 'The translations were made by the poet himself,' Hughes wrote. 'All I did was correct the more intrusive oddities and errors of grammar and usage, and in some places shift about the phrasing and line endings. What I wanted to preserve above all was the tone and cadence of Amichai's own voice speaking in English which seems to me marvellously true to the poetry, in these renderings.'*]

Correspondence between Hughes and Amichai

TH to YA (1970?): The poems arrived – beautiful [the *Selected Poems of Yehuda Amichai*, Penguin, 1971, was in preparation]. When I read your poems I get the feeling poems are waiting everywhere and ready to be made out of anything – wonderful sense of richness and abundance. There are just a few places where the English is obscure or too roundabout. I'll go through it in detail and send you a list of my queries.

TH to YA (June 1975): The BBC has agreed to do a 30 minute programme of your poems, Yehuda. [. . .] Whoever I've shown them to is really hard hit by them. They seem looser than your earlier poems – but bigger & heavier. As though your real life needs looser pants than formerly. They are a different sort of poetry than anything else I know – they make everything set against them seem 'literary'. Some of them make me realise that I – for instance – have neglected the real thing – perhaps because it seems too near. Perhaps too near for my telescopic sights to see it at all. Though I know it's really all I want to write about, & all I really want to read.

YA to TH (17 July 1975): As to your remarks about my poems, it's strange that I feel towards your poems that they are real and concentrated like a land-mine un-exploded but filled with power [. . .] Whereas I feel about my things sometimes that they are like a mine *after* the explosion: scattered pieces, words, experiences, all strewn openly around for everyone to see – I was happy that you are doing a BBC program on them. I hope you worked a bit on my rough translation . . .

TH to YA (November 1975): You'll have been wondering what's happened to your poems [. . .] I've gone through them carefully. My problem is – that your translation has an idiom, and a tone, which is exactly you & which is very powerful poetry in itself, but which is just slightly strange in English [. . .] The English of your translation is more like the English of somebody – some English body – with no literary education. Unspoiled, whole, life-size, natural etc. And with the oddity which is really you; so I want to keep that. The whole warm, living impact of the poems depends on that. I saw 2 or 3 of your poems in a magazine, where you had altered them more, anglicised them more, made them more 'correct', but it seemed to me you'd knocked out some of the natural animal life – which the translations you sent me *all* have. So, I've simply corrected gross foreignisms. Otherwise, I've altered nothing . . .

YA to TH (11 July 1977): Gaudete arrived in a heat wave in Jerusalem [. . .] making me forget heat and political heat with a power I haven't experienced a long time. I saw North Tawton and the way you said that under all this gentle greenery there are mounds and blood and wild prehistoric doings – So strange that after reading and reading it I had the feeling that I try to do the opposite in my things. Finding under all the burning [. . .] a mystery of this country, some sweetness, gentleness [. . .]. We should change places for some time . . .

TH to YA (1982): What a translator needs is pure calm – no distortions even of air-current or water-currents. Also can he [here he names another translator of YA's poetry] transmit your unique inflection – only you can do that . . .

TH to YA (14 May 1983): I read it [proofs of a book by YA that had arrived from America] with my usual total joy and satisfaction. Yehuda, I think you are my favourite poet – on one side there are all modern poets, writing the great intercontinental express of modern poetry, coaches crammed indiscriminately with great men, brilliant women, comedians, charlatans, ninnies, etc., but all racing along the flashing rails, in a resounding 150 mph concatenation of modern poetry, hurtling through the century, and on the other side is you – absolutely alone and apart from them – standing I imagine on a dusty hill over Jerusalem – the sole shepherd of the voices of human beings. You've discovered a subject that seems absolutely new to poetry, and it turns out to be the human being speaking like a human being about being a human being, or rather singing like one. The undiscovered animal!

APPENDIX 7 Seneca

Literal version by Frank Justus Miller
(See *Seneca VIII, Tragedies I* Cambridge, Mass., 1979; London, The Loeb Classical Library, 1917)
   (*Oedipus calls for the crime unwittingly committed by himself to be avenged.*)

Now at Heaven's command let the crime be expiated.
Whoever of the gods dost look with favour upon kingdoms – though, thou whose are the laws of the swift-revolving heavens; and thou, greatest glory of the unclouded sky, who presidest over the twelve signs in thy changing course, who dost unroll the slow centuries with swift wheel; and thou, his sister, ever faring opposite to thy brother, Phoebe, night-wanderer; thou whom the winds obey, who over the level deep dost speed thy azure car; and thou who dost allot homes devoid of light – do ye all attend [. . .]

Version by David Anthony Turner
(*Classical Tragedy: Greek and Roman: Eight Plays*, New York, 1990)

Well, the Gods demand it. Now someone will pay for that atrocity. All you gods who look kindly on the work of kings, be near me. May no house be a haven, no home secure, may no country welcome in his banishment the man whose hand struck down King Laius. May shame torment his bed, may his seed mock heaven. With that same hand may he kill even his own father, and may he – can any curse he more deadly? – may he do all the things I have escaped. There shall be no forgiveness anywhere. Apollo who moves the lips of the priestess to speak the future, come yourself as witness to my words. By the kingdom here of which I am guest, and master, by the gods of that home I left behind – I make this oath. My father, and a quiet old age for him, peaceful possession of a high majesty till death, for Merope my mother – marriage to Polybus only, never to – someone else . . . On all this may mercy for the guilty man depend. May I not spare him . . .

But the scene of that foul murder – where did it take place? Tell me again. Was it a fair fight or an ambush?

Version by Alexander Nevyle

(From *Oedipus, The Fifth Tragedy of Seneca* (1560) by Alexander Nevyle: see The Tudor Translations, second series, 1927, Volume II, *Seneca His Tenne Tragedies*, translated into English, edited by Thomas Newton, anno 1581, with an Introduction by T. S. Eliot to Volume I.)

(Alexander Nevyle (1544–1614) states, in his Dedication, that he translated Oedipus *to be acted at Cambridge. He was only sixteen at the time.)*

> Let us (sith God commaunds) forthwith some good
>   atonement make
> If any way, or means there be their wrathful rage to slake.
> Thou God that sits on seate on high, and all the world dost
>   guide,
> And thou by whose commaundment the Starres in Skies do
>   glide:
> Thou, thou that onely ruler art of Seas, of Floods, and all,
> On thee and on thy Godhead great, for these requestes I
>   call.
> Who so hath slayne king Laius, oh Jove I do thee pray,
> Let thousand ills upon him fall, before his dying day.
> Let him no health ne comfort have, but al to crusht with
>   cares,
> Consume his wretched yeares in griefe, and though that
>   Death him spares
> Awhyle. Yet mischiefes all, at length uppon him light.
> With all the evile under Sun, that ugly monster smight.
> In exile let him live a Slave, the rated course of life.
> In shame, in care, in penury, in daunger and in strife.
> Let no man on him pity take, let all men him revile.
> Let him his Mothers sacred Bed incestuously defile.
> Let him his father kill. And yet let him do mischiefes . . .

APPENDIX 8 János Pilinszky

Excerpt from Hughes's Introduction to *Selected Poems*

Very many lines of his [Csokits's] rough draft have been impossible to improve, as far as I could judge, and besides that odd inevitability and 'style' which a poet's translation into language other than his own often seems to have, he retained naturally an unspoiled sense of the flavour and the tone of the originals – that very intriguing quality which is the translator's will-o'-the-wisp, the foreignness and strangeness.

Janós Csokits's version of 'The French Prisoner'
(*The final two stanzas only are printed here. In addition, Csokits provided Hughes with contextual notes, not reproduced here.*)

Go on with this – what for? Guards came for him;
he had escaped from the near-by prisoners' camp.
And I am wandering about, as I did in that garden then,
among the shadows of this garden at home.
I look into my notes and quote:
'If only I could forget him, that Frenchman . . .'
And from my ears, my eyes, my mouth
the fierce memory fervently shouts at me:

'I am hungry!' And all at once I feel that immortal hunger
    which
the poor wretch does not feel since long,
and which no earthly food can still.
He lives on me! And ever more hungrily!
And I am less and less enough for him!
He who would have subsisted on any aliment:
is demanding now my heart.

APPENDIX 9 Marin Sorescu

Literal version of 'The Whistle' by Joanna Russell-Gebbett

A whistle shrieks suddenly
Behind a passer-by
Whose body fills up with saw-dust
Like a tree, when it feels

At the edge of the forest
The saw.

Nonetheless, let's not turn my head – the man says to
    himself –
Maybe it's for someone else.
Anyway, let's have a respite
Of some more steps.

The whistle is heard stridently
Behind all the passers-by
Who become purple, yellow, green, red
And walk forwards stiffly
Without turning their heads.
Maybe it's for someone else –
Everyone thinks –
What have I done, but [?]
One war, two wars?
Tomorrow I've the wedding,
The day after tomorrow my wife will give birth,
In two days time I bury my parents –
I've so many things to do,
It can't be for me.

A child
Bought himself a whistle,
And went out to try it
On the boulevard,
Whistling cheekily in people's ears.

APPENDIX 10   Camillo Pennati

Pennati's English original of 'Seascape'

> Waves into waves their streaming manes
> unfolding seas of immemorial time
> driving the rain from foggy and stormy
> billowing of clouds till air from its turmoil
> thus blind clears into a silken gaze
> quivering upon an endless hue of colours

deep on reflecting elements of depths
now that the heaving swell subsides
to a breathing lull of everchanging
scales the foamy crests to sailing
glitters beaming the effusive light
like topmost leaves of forests though made
of water over its fluid expanse of streaming
green or blue far into the utmost outlines
or rimming where the shore outlines
its dizzy or gently sloping end
within the attraction and the atmospheric
gravity of down to earth existence happening
as time itself is spanning into so many
shapes of life into so many shapes of sudden
beauty reflecting with the insight of light
all their embrace that quivers into shades
from where they breathe partaking of a share
of space as leafing through their volume
into the illuminated page of time

Pennati's translation of 'Seascape' ('Paesaggio marino')
into Italian

Onde dopo onde in schiumanti criniere
a svolgere mari di tempo immemorabile
a spingere la pioggia da un nebuloso e perturbato
attorcersi di nubi finché l'aria dal suo tumulto
cosí accecata sí sgombra in un serico sguardo
ondulante sopra un'illimitata sfumatura di colori
fondi a riflettere elementi di profondo spessore
ora che il ribollire turbolento
cede ad un alito cullante di infinite scaglie
le schiumeggianti creste
a veleggianti luminii irraggianti l'effusiva luce
come le alte foglie di foreste anche se consistenti
d'acqua sulla sua fluida vastità di verde
che fluttua o blu là verso l'estremo lembo della vista
o a bordare la costa dove contorna
il suo vertiginoso o digradante termine

addentro l'attrazione e l'atmosferica gravità
dell'esistenza raso terra nel suo accadere intanto
che lo stesso tempo si scandisce in cosí tante forme
dell'esistere in cosí tante forme
d'improvvisa bellezza nel suo riflettersi all'intuito
della luce tutto quell'abbracciante fremere di ombre
da dove condividono il respiro con una parte
dello spazio come sfogliando il proprio del volume
del tempo in una pagina miniata.

Letter from Hughes to Pennati: (10 August 1989)

Dear Camillo,

Here are all the pieces. They make sense to me, and they read O.K.

First, I took them some way from your originals. But gradually, I came to feel that close & literal loyalty – even where it seemed slightly odd – was preferable.

I sense very strongly the slightly deadpan oblique angle of your observations, and the particular medium – the mix of verbal & syntactic chemicals – in which you precipitate your designs. And looking at the Italian I can physically see the moulded concentration of your statements. Those qualities cannot be imposed on a given chunk of language – as a translator can only impose. They can only be exuded with the original expression from the original mind. As you know.

Still I think in these versions one can feel very strongly that they are – the originals – real poems.

Send them back with any notes of your dissatisfactions.

APPENDIX 11 Lorenzo de' Medici

Note by Gaia Servadio

TH decided to discard all existing translations and start afresh. In the British Library I found various Edwardian and Victorian versions, which I photocopied and sent to him; he didn't like any of them. Lorenzo's poetry was out of fashion in England at that time, because of its enthusiastic, happy nature i.e. the very opposite of the punitive, puritan, Victorian manner.

At the Accademia Italiana [I was given] the literary side. I enjoyed setting up my own literary programme. I did some 'classi dantiste' (Dante classes) and tried to organise discussions on libretti and opera. I also devised a celebration of Italian poetry as interpreted or translated by a number of major contemporary English-language poets. I would read the Italian original at the event and the English guest poet would read the translation; after this there would be a question-and-answer session and some further discussion.

Each poet, of course, made changes in the texts I chose. Robert Lowell read his 'Imitations' of Leopardi and Dante. An evening was dedicated to Primo Levi's poetry, with contributions by Al Alvarez. He and I translated several poems, which we read, and *The New Yorker* then published them. Grey Gowrie read Montale; Stephen Spender Petrarch, and there was a number of other memorable readings.

[. . .] [I]t must have been in 1992 that I wrote to Ted Hughes whom I didn't know and who I was convinced would reject or ignore the proposal. Instead he was interested, perhaps because at the time he was engrossed with Renaissance (English) poetry. We talked on the phone and then met; I was to do the selection (Lorenzo's poetic oeuvre is immense). After attempting to represent the diversity of Lorenzo's work – a sonnet on the death of Simonetta, a bawdy song, his most famous Ballata etc. – I looked for existing translations of those poems. It was then that TH asked me instead if I would translate them word-for-word myself. I would type one stanza and underneath it an ad verbum version; if the result still seemed obscure, I would attempt to clarify it by offering alternative words or phrasings, in parentheses. TH would then rework the versions. Occasionally, he had problems with a particular word (e.g. happy, pleased, gay, oblivious) and I would simply let him know which one seemed right to me.

I remember how impressed I was, at this stage, by his familiarity with the work of Ficino and Plotinus and all those philosophers around the Medicean dinner-table. He knew about Lorenzo's teacher Poliziano and about Alberti. I was surprised how quickly he caught the tone of each poem, these being famously diverse, in mood, subject and literary expression.

Interlinear version of Sonetto IX by Gaia Servadio

> *Quanto sia vana ogni speranza nostra,*
>   How vain is every hope of ours
> *quanto fallace ciaschedun disegno,*
>   how whimsical each design
> *quanto sia il mondo d'ignoranza pregno,*
>   how the world is full of ignorance
> *la maestra di tutto, Morte, il mostra.*
>   the master of all, Death, shows.
>
> *Altri si vive in canti e in ballli e in giostra,*
>   There are those who live singing and dancing and for
>   parties

altri a cosa gentil muove lo ingegno,
> others' minds are moved by gentle matters

altri il mondo ha, e le sue cose, a sdegno,
> others keep the world and its matters in contempt

altri quel che drento ha, fuor non dimostra.
> others what they have inside, do not show outside.

Vane cure e pensier, diverse sorte
> Vain worries and thoughts, different fortunes

per la diversita' che da' Natura,
> for the diversity given by Nature

si vede ciascun tempo al mondo errante.
> each time sees us wander in the world.

Ogni cosa e' fugace e poco dura,
> Everything is fleeting and lasts a short time

tanto Fortuna al mondo e' mal constante;
> since Fortune in the world is a constant ill;

solo sta ferma e sempre dura Morte.
> only is still and always lasts Death.

APPENDIX 12 Ovid

Line-by-line modern version by D. E. Hill (Ovid, *Metamorphoses*, I–IV, 1985)

> 'I have won, and he is mine,' cried out the Naiad, and she
>> threw all her clothing well away from her and rushed into
>> the middle of the waters
>
> and held him as he fought against her, violently snatching
>> kisses
>
> and bringing her hands up under him and touching his
>> unwilling breast;
>
> and now she draped herself around the youth this way and
>> that.
>
> At last, though he struggled against her in his desire to get
>> away,
>
> she entwined herself around him like a snake picked up by
>> the king of birds

and snatched aloft (as she hangs from him she binds his head
and feet and entwines her tail around his spreading wings),
or like ivy which likes to weave its way up tall tree trunks,
or like an octopus catching and holding its enemy
beneath the sea by spreading its tentacles in all directions.

APPENDIX 13 Aeschylus

Version (partially rhyming) by Philip Vellacott of part of Excerpt 1
(page 125)

> I am the man to speak, if you would hear
> The whole tale from its hopeful starting place –
> That portent, which amazed our marching youth.
> It was ten years ago – but I was there.
> The poet's grace, the singer's fire,
> Grow with his years; and I can still speak truth
> With the clear ring the gods inspire; –
> How those twin monarchs of our warlike race,
> Two leaders one in purpose, were sped forth –
> Their vengeful spears in thousands pointing North
> To Troy – by four wings' furious beat;
> Two kings of birds, that seemed to bode
> Great fortune to the kings of that great fleet.
> Close to the palace, on spear-side of the road,
> One tawny-feathered, one white in the tail,
> Perched in full view, they ravenously tear
> The body of a pregnant hare
> Big with her burden, now a living prey
> In the last darkness of their unborn day.

Version by Hugh Lloyd-Jones of the first part of Excerpt 1
(Duckworth, 2001; first published, 1982)

> I have power to tell of the auspicious command of the
>   expedition, the command of men
> in authority; for still from the gods am I inspired
> With persuasive power, my strength in song, by the life that
>   has grown up with me:

To tell how the two-throned command of the Achaeans, of
   the youth of Hellas
the concordant leadership,
was sped with avenging spear and arm
by the warlike bird of omen to the Teucrian land,
the king of birds appearing to the kings of the ships,
the black eagle and behind it the white one,
appearing near the palace on the hand in which the spear is
   brandished,
in seats conspicuous,
feeding upon the hare, her womb teeming with young,
checked from running her final course.

APPENDIX 14 Abdulah Sidran

Hughes to Chris Agee (30 November 1997)

I have had a shot at six of the Sidran. I certainly do sense what they must be in
the original, but the difficulty – from my point of view – is that his procedure
is so focused and simple, almost plain, so precise, that any deviation from his
literal words feels simultaneously like a violation (pointless and stupid) and a
dilution. The possibility of feeding some kind of intensity back into the literal
cribs is therefore limited almost entirely to syntactic shifts – mostly a matter of
controlling the pace, the timing. Luckily (I thought) Antonela's cribs are
extremely good – richly toned and lucid at the same time. Anyway, I don't
think I can do much more with these and so they remain, as far as vocabulary
and ideas go, pretty well as literal as they can be. For me, as I say, they enable
me to imagine what the original must be like.

Even so, it's the kind of poetry, I suspect, that loses a lot in translation – that
in the original depends heavily on vocal tone, syllabic saturation in the mari-
nade of the poet's own make-up, the special quality and temper and musical
structure, so to speak, of his unique nature. Untranslatable, all that. The way
the greatness, power etc. of a singer has nothing much to do, really, with the
song – melody and words that any fool could sing.

Literal translation of 'Gavrilo' by Antonela Glavinic

This night is unreal, quiet like hell
which does not exist. The world, houses and things
submerged in oil. The right time for the
   indecisive/hesitating:

you (one) need(s)/should/ought to descend/go down the
    rotten staircase,
you need to touch that wall with your hand, that oil,
you need to say: let's go, sweetheart/soul, to get the
    weapons! For,

so unreal and too quiet is this/the night. There is no
one to tell us: Tomorrow, horror awaits you!
Tomorrow, love awaits you! The skull fills/is filling
with terrible light. Let's hurry, soul/sweetheart,
to get the weapons before the bone cracks from that
    brightness!
Somewhere near-by a true shield is being
    forged/hammered . . .

APPENDIX 15 Alexander Pushkin

Word-for-word version of 'The Prophet' by Valentina Polukhina and
Daniel Weissbort

With-spiritual thirst wearied/worn-down,
In a-desert/wilderness dark/sombre I dragged-myself-along,
And a-six-winged seraphim
On/at the-cross-roads to-me appeared.
With-fingers light like a-dream/sleep
My eye-pupils touched he;
[Opened] the-prophetic eye-pupils,
As of [belonging to] a-frightened/startled eagle.
My ears touched he,
And them filled noise and ringing/sound:
And heard I of-the-sky the-shuddering,
And the-celestial of-angels flight,
And of-reptiles/creatures the-underwater
    procession/progress,
And of-the-earthly/terrestrial vine the-vegetation/ing.
And he to lips my pressed,
And tore-out sinful/culpable my tongue,
And idly-loquacious and cunning,
And the-sting of-a-wise snake

Into lips frozen mine
Inserted with-right-hand bloody.
And he to-me the-breast clove with-a-sword,
And the-heart palpitating drew-forth,
and a-coal, blazing with-fire,
Into the-breast opened inserted.
Like a-corpse in the-desert/wilderness I lay,
And of-god the-voice to me called out:
'Arise, prophet, and see [arch], and hear,
Fill with-will mine [carry out my will]
And passing-/wandering-by seas and lands,
With-the-word burn the-hearts of-people'.

Literal version of 'The Prophet' by Valentina Polukhina and Daniel
Weissbort

Tormented/Worn down/Wearied by spiritual thirst,
In a sombre/gloomy wilderness/desert I dragged myself
    along,
And a six-winged seraph/seraphim
Appeared to me at the cross-roads.
With fingers light as a dream
He touched the pupils of my eyes.
The prophetic pupils, as of a frightened/startled eagle
    opened.
He touched my ears,
And noise/uproar and a [ringing] sound filled them:
And I heard the shudder[ing] of the heavens/sky,
And the celestial flight of angels,
And the under-water procession/progress/course of sea
    reptiles,
and the vegetation/ing of the earthly/terrestrial vine.
And he pressed himself to my lips,
And tore out my sinful/culpable tongue,
My idly loquacious and crafty/cunning tongue,
And with a bloody right hand,
He inserted the sting of a wise snake
Between my frozen lips.
And he clove my breast with his sword,

And drew forth my palpitating heart,
And into the open breast he inserted
A coal, blazing with fire.
I lay like a corpse in the desert/wilderness,
And the voice of God called out to me/summoned me:
'Arise, prophet, and see, and hear,
Carry out my will,
And passing by sea and land,
Burn the hearts of people with the word.'

Bibliography

Where selections have not been taken from published translations, either the individual collections listed below or Hughes's contributions to collections by diverse hands (e.g., to *Scar on the Stone: Contemporary Poetry from Bosnia*, edited by Chris Agee, Bloodaxe, 1998), they are from unpublished typescripts or manuscripts, mostly in the Ted Hughes archive in Special Collections at Emory University, Atlanta.

Aeschylus, *The Oresteia of Aeschylus*, in a version by Ted Hughes (London: Faber and Faber, 1999)

Amichai, Yehuda, *Selected Poems*, translated by Assia Gutmann and Harold Schimmel with the collaboration of Ted Hughes (Harmondsworth: Penguin Books, 1971)

Amichai, Yehuda, *Time*, translated by the author with Ted Hughes (London: Oxford University Press, 1974)

Amichai, Yehuda, *Amen*, translated by the author and Ted Hughes (New York: Harper & Row, 1977, 1979)

Euripides, *Alcestis*, in a new version by Ted Hughes (London: Faber and Faber, 1999)

Lorca, Federico García, *Lorca's Blood Wedding*, in a version by Ted Hughes (London: Faber and Faber, 1996)

Ovid, *Tales from Ovid: Twenty-four Passages from the Metamorphoses*, translated by Ted Hughes (London: Faber and Faber, 1997)

Pilinszky, János, *János Pilinszky: Selected Poems*, translated by Ted Hughes and János Csokits (Manchester: Carcanet, 1977, and New York: Persea Books, 1977); reissued as *The Desert of Love* (London: Anvil, 1989)

Racine, Jean, *Racine's Phèdre*, in a new version by Ted Hughes (London: Faber and Faber, 1998)

Schehadé, Georges, *The Story of Vasco*, opera in three acts, music by Gordon Crosse, libretto based on an English version by Ted Hughes of the play *L'Histoire de Vasco* by Georges Schehadé (London: Oxford University Press, 1974)

Seneca, *Seneca's Oedipus*, adapted by Ted Hughes (London: Faber and Faber, 1969)

Wedekind, Frank, *Wedekind's Spring Awakening*, in a new version by Ted Hughes (London: Faber and Faber, 1995)

Acknowledgments

The editor gratefully acknowledges the help of Carol Hughes, particularly with respect to Ted Hughes's draft translation of *Sir Gawain and the Green Knight* but also for permitting him to study the various typescript drafts of Hughes's translation of Racine's *Phèdre* and in general for allowing him to browse in Ted Hughes's library before it was shipped to Emory University, as well as making him aware of what *Orghast* actually sounded like in performance. Olwyn Hughes, Ted Hughes's sister, also commented very helpfully on the editor's remarks and surmises about the translations. Thanks are likewise due to Stephen Enniss, director of special collections at the Woodruff Library at Emory University, Atlanta, and to his staff. Most of Ted Hughes's notebooks and papers, including many draft translations, are located at Emory, and every effort was made to make the editor's stay productive and agreeable and to help him find what he was looking for in the notebooks and other papers meticulously preserved by Hughes, as well as in the latter's voluminous and detailed correspondence, a selection of which, edited by Christopher Reid, will shortly be published by Faber. The editor is similarly indebted to Paul Keegan, for *The Collected Poems*, which of course provides the essential context for the translations and which, besides, includes some translational work, e.g., Hughes's one translation of Homer, reproduced also in the present volume. Charles Boyle, copy-editor at Faber, gave the editor the benefit of his advice and experience, extremely useful at a comparatively early and crucial stage in the preparation of this manuscript. Thanks are due to a number of other individuals who gave unstintingly of their time and experience, including Hana Amichai (re Yehuda Amichai), Neil Astley (re Sorescu), Jonathan Kent (re Racine), Tim Supple (re Lorca and Ovid), Lucas Myers, a contemporary of Ted Hughes and of the editor at Cambridge (re the *Bardo*), Helder and Suzette Macedo (re Portuguese poetry and Helder Macedo's poetry), A.C.H. Smith (re *Orghast*), Gaia Servadio (re Lorenzo de' Medici), Keith Sagar (re *Sir Gawain*), and last but not least, my wife, Valentina Polukhina, who drafted and annotated a literal translation of Pushkin's poem "The Prophet" for Ted Hughes, this translation being, in fact, his last poem. Apologies are extended to others whose names are perhaps not mentioned here. In general, everybody approached was ready and willing. This collection would have been inconceivable without the help and support of many generous individuals.

Index

Permissions Acknowledgements

Grateful acknowledgement is made for permission to reprint the following material:

Excerpts from the *Oresteia* by Aeschylus, a new version by Ted Hughes (London: Faber and Faber), copyright © The Estate of Ted Hughes, 1999. Nineteen lines from *The Oresteian Trilogy: Agamemnon, The Choephori, The Eumenides* by Aeschylus, translated by Philip Vellacott (Penguin Classics, 1956), copyright © Philip Vellacott, 1956. Version by Hugh Lloyd-Jones of the first part of Excerpt 1 from the *Oresteia* published by Gerald Duckworth & Co. Ltd.

Excerpts from *Yehuda Amichai: Selected Poems*, edited by Ted Hughes and Daniel Weissbort (London: Faber and Faber), copyright © Daniel Weissbort and Ted Hughes, 2000; reproduced by kind permission of the Estate of Yehuda Amichai.

Excerpts from *Sir Gawain and the Green Knight*, by Anonymous (The *Pearl* Poet), from *The School Bag*, edited by Ted Hughes and Seamus Heaney (London: Faber and Faber), copyright © Seamus Heaney and The Estate of Ted Hughes, 1997.

Excerpts from *Du Mouvement et de l'immobilité de Douve* by Yves Bonnefoy copyright © Mercure de France, 1986.

Excerpts from *Choix de poèmes* by Paul Eluard copyright © Éditions Gallimard, three editions, 1941. Other Paul Eluard excerpts from the following collections: *Les Nécessités de la vie* copyright © Gallimard, 1921; *Les nuits partagées* copyright © Gallimard, 1935; *Médieuses* copyright © Gallimard, 1939; and *La saison des amours* copyright © Gallimard, 1949. Citations used were from the Hughes papers and consulted while the papers were in private hands, copyright © The Estate of Ted Hughes.

Excerpts from *Alcestis* by Euripides, translated by Ted Hughes (London: Faber and Faber), copyright © The Estate of Ted Hughes, 1999.

Excerpts from the *Odyssey* by Homer, translated by Ted Hughes, from *Ted Hughes: Collected Poems* (London: Faber and Faber), copyright © The Estate of Ted Hughes, 2003.

Poetry International 1967 programme note by Ted Hughes copyright © The Estate of Ted Hughes.

PERMISSIONS ACKNOWLEDGEMENTS

'The Boy Changed into a Stag Cries out at the Gate of Secrets' by Ferenc Juhász, translated by Ted Hughes (first published in *Modern Poetry in Translation*, Number 21, 2003), reproduced with kind permission of the editors of *Modern Poetry in Translation*. Excerpt from Kenneth McRobbie's version of the poem from *The Plough and the Pen*, edited by Ilona Duczynska and Karl Polanyi, 1963, reproduced with kind permission of Peter Owen Ltd, London. Excerpt from David Wevill's version from *Selected Poems of Sandor Weores* and Ferenc Juhász (Penguin, 1970). Reproduced with the kind permission of David Wevill. Excerpts from *Modern Poetry in Translation* (Number 1, 1965; Number 3, 1967; and Introduction, 1982) reproduced with kind permission of the editors of *Modern Poetry in Translation*.

Excerpts from *Blood Wedding* (London: Faber and Faber) by Federico García Lorca, translated by Ted Hughes, copyright © The Estate of Ted Hughes, 1996. Excerpts from 'The Old Lizard', 'Ballad of the Water of the Sea', 'The Interrupted Concert', and 'Poem of the Saeta', from the Manuscript, Archives, and Rare Book Library, Emory University and copyright © The Estate of Ted Hughes.

'When the mirror is broken open' by Helder Macedo and letters from Ted Hughes to Helder and Suzette Macedo and from Suzette Macedo to Daniel Weissbort reproduced with kind permission of Helder and Suzette Macedo.

Excerpts from *Tales from Ovid* (London: Faber and Faber) copyright © The Estate of Ted Hughes, 1997. Translation of Ovid's *Metamorphoses* by D. E. Hill reproduced by permission of Aris & Phillips from *Ovid: Metamorphoses I–IV*, edited with an introduction, translation and commentary by D. E. Hill, Aris & Phillips, 1985.

Camillo Pennati's English original of 'Seascape' and translation of 'Seascape' ('Paesaggio marino'), copyright © Camillo Pennati, and extract from a letter from Ted Hughes to Camillo Pennati, 10 August 1989, both reproduced with kind permission of Camillo Pennati.

'Harbach', 'The French Prisoner', 'On the Wall of a KZ-Lager', 'Passion of Ravensbrück', 'Impromptu', 'The Desert of Love', 'Unfinished Past', 'Van Gogh', 'The Passion' and 'The Prayer of Van Gogh' are taken from *János Pilinszky: The Desert of Love*, translated by János Csokits and Ted Hughes, Anvil Press Poetry, 1989.

Word-for-word and literal versions of 'The Prophet' by Alexander Pushkin reproduced with kind permission of Daniel Weissbort and Valentina Polukhina.

Excerpts from *Phèdre* by Jean Racine, translated by Ted Hughes (London: Faber and Faber), copyright © The Estate of Ted Hughes, 1998.

Mário de Sá Carneiro: citations used from the Hughes papers and consulted